WHY THE SKY IS BLUE

& OTHER WONDERS OF THE EARTH

WHY THE SKY IS BLUE

& OTHER WONDERS OF THE EARTH

WILLIAM CLEVENGER

MALLARD
PRESS

A FRIEDMAN GROUP BOOK

Published by MALLARD PRESS
An Imprint of BDD Promotional Book Company, Inc.
666 Fifth Avenue
New York, N.Y. 10103

Mallard Press and its accompanying design and logo are trademarks of BDD Promotional
Book Company, Inc.

ISBN 0–7924–5746-3

WHY THE SKY IS BLUE AND OTHER WONDERS OF THE EARTH
was prepared and produced by
Michael Friedman Publishing Group, Inc.
15 West 26th Street
New York, New York 10010

Editors: Sharon Kalman and Kelly Matthews
Art Direction: Devorah Levinrad
Designer: Judy Morgan
Photography Editor: Christopher C. Bain
Illustrations: Irina Pomerantzeff

Typeset by Classic Type, Inc.
Color separations by Rainbow Graphic Arts Co.
Printed and bound in Hong Kong by Leefung-Asco Printers Ltd.

ACKNOWLEDGMENTS

Thanks to Joe, LeeAnn, Jeanie, and Jerry Dunn, and Dave Carlstrom for encouragement and useful suggestions. Special thanks to Kathy Wright for proofreading the manuscript and to Lorianne for a truly "phenomenal" research effort. Also my sincere gratitude goes out to Sharon Kalman and Kelly Matthews for orchestrating this project.

DEDICATION

This one's for Chris, the most amazing work of nature I know.

T A B L E   O F

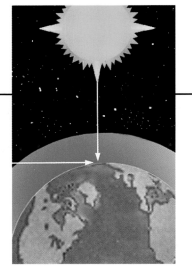

CONTENTS

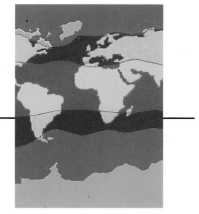

INTRODUCTION

Curiosity, it seems to me, is primarily a human trait. Animals do not spend much time puzzling over things—as far as I can tell—especially not cats, the old adage notwithstanding. But as far back as history records, people have wondered about the world around them and the universe beyond. We harbor an innate desire to understand the phenomena we observe and how they work.

This desire to figure out things sets in at an early age. The four-year-old children I know are best described as "question marks with legs" because they spend a good portion of their time firing out steady barrages of inquiries and following you around until satisfactory answers are obtained. As we grow up, the business of living often puts a damper on our natural inquisitiveness, but occasionally even grown-ups, when they have a moment to

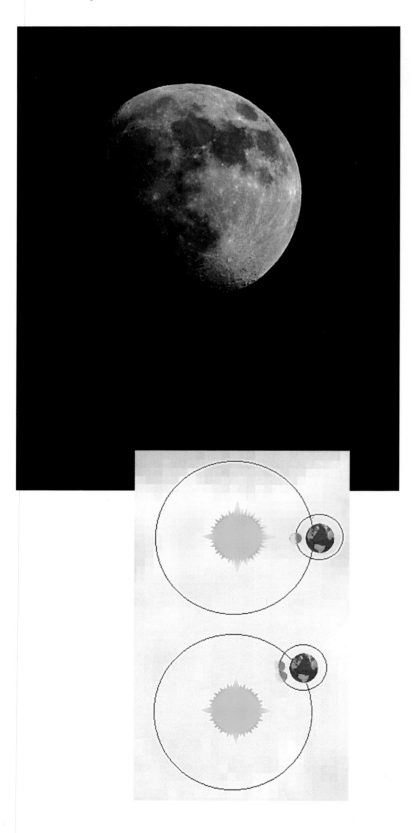

relax, are taken in by some spectacle of nature, something as simple as the majestic sky above, and that childhood curiosity is triggered again: Why is the sky blue?

In this book, I attempt to explain the scientific basis for some of the natural phenomena we observe in the world around us. The questions were easy to come up with—I have three very inquisitive children of my own.

This is by no means an exhaustive treatment of the chosen topics; in fact, weighty volumes can be found on every one of these subjects. The goal here was to focus on the mechanisms underlying these phenomena—the whys and hows—and briefly explain the principles by which these observed events can be understood. Such an approach will, I hope, answer questions you may have wondered about from time to time.

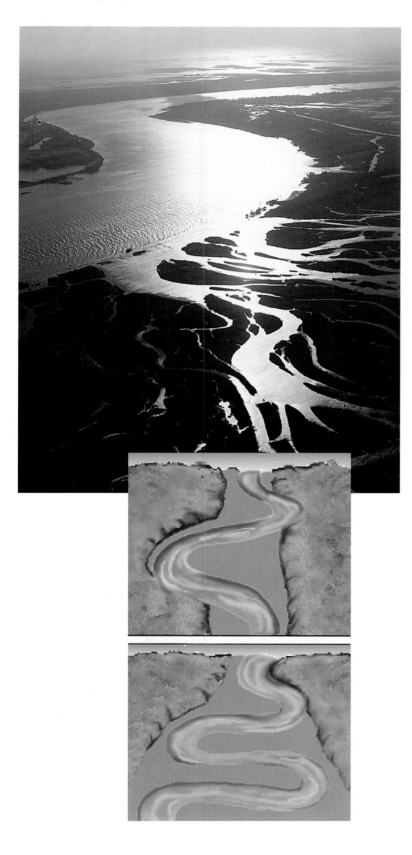

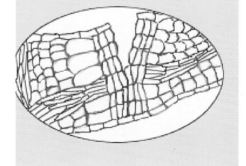

THE SKY AND BEYOND

WHY IS THE SKY BLUE?

WHEN WAS THE LAST TIME you stopped to take a good look at a bright, cloudless sky? There is something innately soothing about that dimensionless screen stretched out above us from horizon to horizon. It provokes a sense of wonder about our world and the universe beyond. And as you gazed out and took in the sight, did you find yourself wondering what gives the sky its rich blue color?

What we observe as the visible daytime sky is the result of sunlight interacting with our atmosphere. To understand this phenomenon, we must first know something about the basic features of these two components, light and air. Then we can understand how they interact to create the blue color we normally see.

Visible light is one example of a type of energy called electromagnetic radiation (Figure 2). There are several other kinds of electromagnetic radiation including gamma rays, x-rays, infrared waves, and radio waves. All of these types of energy are propagated as waves, and the key feature that distinguishes one type from another is wavelength.

The entire spectrum of electromagnetic radiation includes an incredibly large range of wavelengths. The shortest waves are only a few trillionths of an inch (or centimeter) long, while the longest are measured in hundreds of miles (or kilometers). The wavelength of a particular type of electromagnetic radiation is defined as the distance between two successive points in the wave (Figure 1). Visible light includes those wavelengths that measure between 155 to 275 billionths of an inch (400 to 700 nanometers).

Light has many intriguing characteristics. For example, light exhibits properties of both pure energy and material particles. This means that in some ways light behaves like formless radiant energy, as though it has no mass at all. But in other ways it demonstrates activities characteristic of a particle—an actual physical entity. This dual nature of light is interesting and complex, and has been the subject of intense study by physicists for hundreds of years.

Another important property of light is that it always tends to travel in a straight line, unless influenced by some outside force. Also, light can be reflected: It can bounce off of certain kinds of material to travel in another direction. These are important features to keep in mind, since they play a role in what happens to light as it approaches the earth.

Figure 1
WAVELENGTH: The length of a particular type of wave is measured from the crest of one wave to the crest of the next.

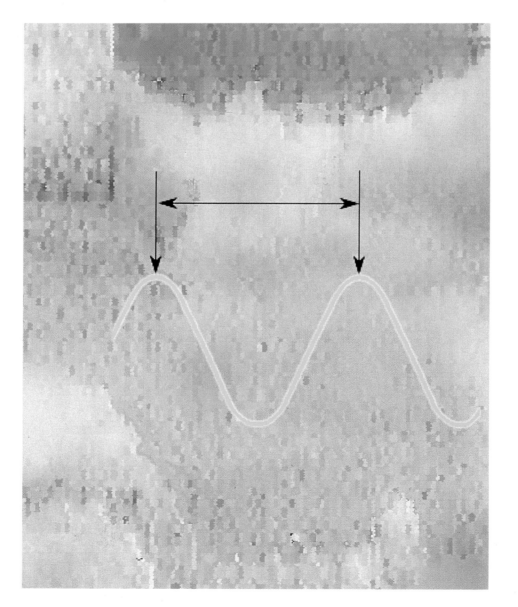

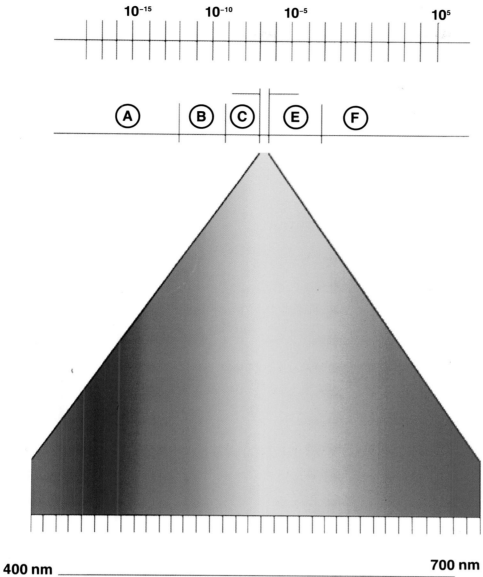

10^{-15} 10^{-10} 10^{-5} 10^{5}

A   B   C   E   F

400 nm   700 nm

**Figure 2
ELECTROMAGNETIC
SPECTRUM:** Different
types of electromagnetic
energy are characterized
by their wavelengths,
which vary greatly in
size and are measured
in meters on the scale
at the top of this figure.
The wavelengths of
various energy forms
are broken down
into A) gamma rays,
B) x-rays; C) ultraviolet;
D) visible; E) infrared;
F) radio waves. Visible
light is only a small
fraction of this energy
spectrum.

Now it is time to examine the basic features of the air around us. The earth's atmosphere is a layer of gaseous matter approximately 90 miles (145 km) thick. It is held in place by the earth's gravitational field. Meteorologists divide our atmosphere into several layers according to its composition (Figure 3). The layer closest to the earth is termed the troposphere and includes approximately the first ten miles (16 km) of air. The next thirty miles (50 km) make up the stratosphere, and the fifty miles (80 km) after that is called the mesosphere. Outside of these three inner layers, which together make up the atmosphere proper, is the ionosphere, measuring 600 miles (960 km) thick, which contains far less gaseous material than the lower regions. The ionosphere also contains charged particles, which play a role in phenomena we will discuss later.

Although we can arbitrarily designate these regions of the atmosphere in order to study them, there is not a clear line that marks the boundaries between them. And there is not a point at which the atmosphere suddenly ends; rather, the air gradually thins out in the highest layer until at some point there are no more gaseous molecules present.

The most abundant gas in our atmosphere is nitrogen, comprising about 78 percent of the total volume. Oxygen is also plentiful at 21 percent. Other notable gases are argon, carbon dioxide, hydrogen, helium, and ozone, which together make up the remaining 1 percent of the air, along with traces of many other substances. The proportion of these gases varies within the layers of the atmosphere, and there is generally less of all of them with increasing distance from the earth. Some are concentrated in specific sections. An example is ozone, which is confined primarily to a thin band in the bottom region of the stratosphere. There is also a significant amount of water vapor in the air, but the concentration varies from place to place and can change rapidly over time.

Figure 3
REGIONS OF THE EARTH'S ATMOSPHERE: The innermost layer is the *troposphere* (A), followed by the *stratosphere* (B), *mesosphere* (C), and *ionosphere* (D).

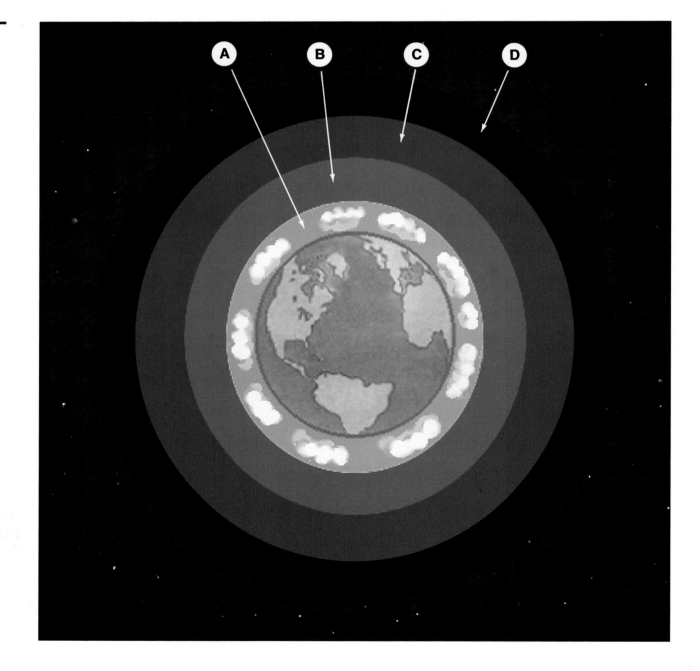

© Stan Osolinski/Dembinsky Photo Association

We are now ready to consider what happens when solar radiation enters the gaseous atmosphere. The white light of the sun, a mixture of all the different colors of visible light, travels toward the earth at incredible speed: 186,000 miles (300,000 m) per second. Even though the sun is 93 million miles (150 million km) away, sunlight traverses this distance in only eight and one-third minutes. Upon its arrival, this light penetrates into the atmosphere and travels toward the earth in a straight line.

If light encounters relatively large particles in the air such as dust or smoke, which are thousands of times larger than the wavelength of light, some of the light will be reflected off in another direction. This phenomenon can be observed in a smoky room with sunlight streaming through a window. You can watch the sunbeams change direction as they reflect off thicker patches of smoke.

A clear sky, however, contains almost no dust or smoke or any other large particles that reflect a substantial amount of sunlight. What a clear sky *does* contain, though, is gases. These gases are very small—approximately one thousand times smaller than the wavelength of visible light. So gases do not directly reflect light, but they do have an effect on it: They *scatter* light.

Scattering is a special kind of interference in which light is reflected in an irregular and diffuse manner. The gaseous molecules alter the course of light and send it off in every possible direction. Different wavelengths of light are not equally affected by air. The shortest wavelengths of sunlight, which are blue in color, are most susceptible to this scattering effect. They bounce all over the sky and enter our eyes from all directions, giving the overall blue impression we observe. The other, longer wavelengths of light are not scattered as much and continue straight down to the earth's surface, where we perceive them as the white sphere of the sun.

It is these scattered, short wavelengths of light that flood our vision when we gaze up and make the sky appear blue.

WHY ARE SUNSETS SO COLORFUL?

TAKING IN A BEAUTIFUL SUNSET at the end of the day is a relaxing and memorable experience. The many striking colors, the diverse shades and tones of pink, orange, purple, and red create a unique scene that stays in our mind long after darkness draws the curtains closed. The sunset, like the blue sky of a bright clear day, is produced when radiant energy from the sun contacts molecules in the atmosphere. But why is the sky so much more colorful under a setting sun compared to the even blue tone we see during most of the day?

Several factors contribute to the picturesque view we observe when the sun approaches the horizon. First, let's consider the fundamental interaction between sunlight and air that causes this event.

The previous section described the phenomenon of scattering, which causes shorter wavelengths of light to diffuse in all directions randomly, producing our perception of the daytime sky as blue. This explains the situation when sunlight travels toward the earth's surface straight on, at a nearly perpendicular angle. At the end of the day, however, what we observe is sunlight streaming toward us from a very low position in the sky—an angle that is almost horizontal (Figure 4). The light that reaches our eyes has passed through considerably more atmosphere than the rays of the noonday sun.

As the various colors of sunlight pass through this increased distance of air, the blue wavelengths are scattered to such an extent that few of them reach us. At the same time, the longer wavelengths of light, including orange and red, penetrate this larger volume of air. But by the time they reach our eyes, these wavelengths have now encountered enough atmospheric gases to undergo significant scattering. Thus they fill the sky with their brilliant color.

This same principle explains why the setting sun appears to be larger and more diffuse around its perimeter than the mid-day sun. More of its radiant energy is distorted by the longer path through air, and we perceive this bending, diffused light in the form of an enlarged, less distinct sphere.

The primary reason, then, for colorful sunsets is the increased distance light must travel through the atmosphere to reach us. But there are several other factors that contribute to a really top-notch sunset. If you think back to an especially memorable one, it's a good bet there were plenty of clouds around. Clouds are a mixture of water vapor and dust particles. Both of these components have strong influences on light, either reflecting it directly or scattering it. For this reason, it is often the various layers and formations of clouds that display the most brilliant patterns and shades of color as the evening sun sets.

Some of the most spectacular sunsets occur when the air contains large amounts of particulate matter. One source of such atmospheric contamination is forest fires, which can fill the air with smoke and ash. This causes intense coloration of the entire sky, especially when the sun is on the horizon. Volcanoes, which can spew thousands of tons of dirt and dust into the atmosphere, have caused some spectacular sunsets. Windstorms, such as hurricanes, have also provided exceptional sunsets by stirring excessive material up into the atmosphere. Ironically, the colors we observe at sunset are sometimes the result of air pollution. The chemicals pumped into the air by industrial processes can contribute to intense coloration of the waning daylight sky.

Perhaps you've wondered about the other occasion when the sun is near the horizon: sunrise. Why don't we hear more about a picturesque sky occurring when the sun comes up, since according to the above explanation, this event should be just as colorful as sunsets? There may be some reduction of airborne material in the morning sky, since condensation during the night hours may pull dust and other particles out of the air. This cleansing, however, is minimal at best; the fact is that sunrises can be and often are just as magnificent as sunsets. The reason we don't see them as often is simple: Most people don't like to get up early enough to watch.

**Figure 4
SUNLIGHT'S PATH
THROUGH THE
ATMOSPHERE:**
At midday, the sun's direct angle sends light through the minimum amount of atmosphere, but at dusk, the sunlight must pass through more air, an event that increases scattering.

WHAT MAKES RAINBOWS?

IN THE PREVIOUS SECTIONS, we considered some of the ways our atmosphere affects incoming sunlight. Another variation of this phenomenon—perhaps the most striking and beautiful of all—is the rainbow.

Throughout history, rainbows have been the object of much superstition and folklore. Several ancient civilizations, including the Pueblo Indians of the American Southwest, believed that the brightly colored arch they saw in the sky was a bridge between this earthly realm and other supernatural worlds. One of the most famous legends originated in Ireland and places a pot of gold at the end of the rainbow. This story is difficult to prove, since a rainbow moves when you do, making it impossible to ever reach the end of it. Not all beliefs about rainbows are positive, however. Folklore of the African Zulu tribe views the rainbow as an evil spirit.

A rainbow begins when sunlight, a mixture of all the colors of light, hits raindrops in the air. The raindrops, which are relatively large compared to air gases, act as prisms: They split the incoming light into its individual colors. This happens because the special properties of a water droplet bend the different wavelengths of light at slightly different angles. These individual wavelengths then bounce off the curved back surface of the raindrop and exit, not together, but divided into their respective colors: Blue light reflects out at an angle of approximately 40 degrees, red at 42 degrees, and all the other colors appear in between. This effectively separates the light beam out into its full spectrum of colors.

Of course it takes more than one raindrop in the sky to produce a rainbow. The range of colors we see results from sunlight bouncing off many raindrops falling through the sky, forming a "screen" on which the sun can project an image.

A remarkable feature of the rainbow is its distinctly arranged bands of color, always in the same sequence. But since raindrops behave as tiny prisms, each one splitting up the colors, wouldn't we expect to see a scattered array of random colors, rather than the precise order we do in fact observe?

We see discrete sections in a rainbow because individual raindrops reflect only one particular wavelength of light along the narrow path to our eyes. The raindrops in the upper region of a rainbow, though reflecting out all of the colors, are in exactly the right position to send only red wavelengths in our specific direction. The lowest raindrops are at a different angle with respect to the sun, and thus the bottom band results from blue wavelengths radiating toward us.

There are two major requirements, then, for a rainbow to form: rain and sunlight. If these were the only two things necessary, we would expect rainbows to be rather common. But, in fact, rainbows are quite rare. This is because there are other conditions that must also be exactly right in order for rainbows to occur. What else must happen?

We've already seen that precise angles of reflection are important in visualizing a rainbow. Since the original source of light for these reflections is the sun, then the sun must be in exactly the right place in the sky for a rainbow to form. In fact, the sun must be behind us, showering light down toward the sheet of raindrops in front of us at a 42-degree angle relative to our location (Figure 5). Therefore, seeing a rainbow is impossible when the sun is directly overhead or near the horizon.

An obvious inhibitor of rainbows is the fact that when it's raining, which is a requirement for this optical phenomenon, it is often the case that clouds obscure the sun. Indirect light is not sufficient to generate a rainbow—there must be full direct sunlight. Taken together, these restrictions limit the number of rainbows that occur.

When they *do* appear, rainbows always come in a curved shape. This can be understood in terms of the 42-degree-angle requirement. The light causing a rainbow is coming in from one spot, the sun, and is being reflected at a precise angle toward our eyes. Imagine a point to the left or right of the top of the rainbow, and picture that angle: It would be *greater* than 42 degrees. The only way to maintain the 42-degree angle as you move out from the center of the rainbow is to curve the line down into an arch.

The same reasoning explains why a rainbow moves when you do: As your angle in relation to the sun and rain changes, so does the location of the image you see. This is why two people looking at a rainbow will see it in slightly different places.

Although rainbows usually appear as arcs, they can also come in full circles. We don't usually see this, because the sheet of rain that projects our image meets the ground. But from an airplane or a high mountain, completely round rainbows can be observed.

On rare occasions, a double rainbow can be seen in the sky. This occurs when light bounces off the raindrop's curved surface not once but twice before exiting. The angle of refraction in this case is different—51 degrees instead of 42—and places the second rainbow slightly above the first. In addition, the order of the colors of the second rainbow is reversed because of the double reflection. Also, partial rainbows can occur when there is not enough rain to reflect a full arch.

It is possible to make your own rainbow: A vertical lawn sprinkler can be positioned so that a small artificial band of colors appears in the spray. It's not as breathtaking as the real thing, but if you live in a desert and have never seen one in person, it's better than nothing.

Figure 5
CONDITIONS THAT PRODUCE A RAINBOW: For a rainbow to be observed, the sun must be positioned at a 42-degree angle relative to the viewer's location.

42°

© J. Zehrt/FPG International

WHAT IS A MIRAGE?

A MIRAGE IS AN OPTICAL ILLUSION that occurs when sunlight is rerouted in a specific direction. This phenomenon is most often seen in open flat areas, such as deserts. It is yet another variation of how the atmosphere plays tricks with incoming sunlight.

One of the properties of light is that it can be refracted, or bent, when it passes from one medium into another, such as going from air into water. This is why a stick, lowered into a pool of water, seems to bend at the water's surface, with the part in the water appearing to be crooked. The light reflecting up through the water and into your eyes has been refracted.

In the case of a mirage, a light beam's course is altered by passing through masses of air that are warmer or colder than surrounding layers. This is because thermal variation alters the density of particular layers, which then behave as different mediums and cause light passing through them to bend slightly. The result is that mirror images of distant objects appear out of place.

The most common type of mirage is called an *inferior* mirage, when the illusion is "inferior" to or below the real object. It is associated with light moving from cool into warmer air. The result is that an object, such as a palm tree, displays an inverted copy, much like a reflection in a lake (Figure 6). Imagine the direction light would travel if you were the observer, viewing the palm tree. Some of the light reflecting off the object would avoid refraction, entering your eyes to reveal the tree's actual location. But light reflecting off the tree at a lower angle, which normally would not come your way, passes through warmer air near the desert floor, and is bent upward. This light would enter your eyes from a lower angle, causing a replica of the tree to appear, positioned lower than the real object.

The other type of mirage is *superior*, or above the real object. It happens when light passes from warm air into cooler air, bending the light down. This occurs most commonly on oceans, and results in objects below the horizon, such as shorelines, appearing suspended in the air.

Figure 6
CREATION OF A MIRAGE: Light passing through warmer air near the ground is bent upward, creating an inverse image positioned below the actual object.

WHAT CAUSES THE NORTHERN LIGHTS?

© F.J. Baker/Dembinsky Photo Association

THE AURORA BOREALIS (northern dawn) is the name of a rarely seen and intriguing lumination that occurs in the night sky over the earth's northern polar region. It takes the form of brilliant sheets of flickering light, variant in color and sometimes hundreds of miles (or kilometers) long, that appear to flash and change shape rapidly. This display has been described as a wavering curtain of light that seems to flicker and dance across the dark sky. The same kind of activity is observed near the south pole, where it is called the aurora australis (southern dawn).

This phenomenon originates from solar activity. The violent thermal reactions that characterize the sun's environment are sufficiently powerful to continuously fling its outer atmosphere, the corona, out into space at high speed. This is not the visible light and other electromagnetic radiation that was described previously, but actual physical matter—ionized particles and gases—that are given the name *solar wind*. As this solar wind streams out away from the sun and approaches our planet, it encounters the earth's magnetic field, a topic we will now briefly discuss.

It was William Gilbert, a physician who lived in the sixteenth century, who first analyzed our planet's basic magnetic properties. He showed that the characteristics of the lines of force around a small magnet are similar to the earth's magnetic field. Current hypotheses attribute this magnetism to the inner structure of our earth, which is thought to be a dense central core of metallic composition surrounded by a molten layer that circulates slowly around the solid interior. This arrangement

has the effect of magnetizing the core, just as an electric current passed through a wire wrapped around a nail will magnetize the nail. Thus our planet is a large and relatively strong magnet, with its own magnetic field extending outward into space.

The material particles of the solar wind are strongly influenced by the earth's magnetic field. The high-speed ions, mostly electrons, are drawn toward the poles, where they collide with gases in the ionosphere. These collisions result in an electrical discharge, the product of which is the glowing light called the aurora.

Incoming electrons build up sufficient force to excite several hundred gaseous molecules before dissipating in the earth's atmosphere about 60 miles (96 km) above the earth. The typical greenish hue of the aurora is produced by bombarded oxygen atoms, while collisions with nitrogen cause several other colors. Generally this occurs at a latitude of about 67 degrees, making the display visible only from locations close to the north and south poles.

Auroral intensity is linked to solar upheavals. This has allowed scientists to accurately predict auroral activity by monitoring the sun's activity and also by monitoring changes in the solar wind approaching the earth. Exceptionally strong solar flares are followed by strong geomagnetic storms, usually about forty hours later, which increase the intensity and geographical range of auroral events. On occasion, the northern lights expand far enough south to be observed from most parts of the continental United States.

HOW DO SUNSPOTS FORM?

THE SUN RESIDES AT THE CENTER OF our solar system and controls many aspects of the earth's environment. Solar radiation accounts for almost all of the earth's energy, either directly in the form of electromagnetic radiation or indirectly as chemical energy stored in the biomass or as fossil fuels. Without the sun's constant output of light and heat, life on this planet would not exist.

The natural phenomena we have considered thus far all result from some type of solar emanation interacting with our planet and its surrounding atmosphere or magnetic field. But the sun exhibits spectacular phenomena of its own, which can be observed from earth with special photographic techniques. One such event is the formation of large disturbances on the sun's outer surface called sunspots. Let's first review the sun's basic features and structure, and then we will consider the special conditions that cause sunspots.

Astronomers classify our sun as a star—a self-gravitating object that generates its own energy by nuclear processes. Our sun is an average-size star and is just one of over 100 billion stars in the Milky Way Galaxy. The sun is about 93 million miles (150 million km) away from us, and its mass is approximately 330,000 times that of the earth. Our next nearest star,

Alpha Centauri, is over 25 trillion miles (40 trillion km) away, far too distant to have any noticeable effect on this planet.

The sun constantly puts out an incredible amount of energy, about 500 thousand billion billion (5×10^{23}) horsepower. This is roughly equivalent to the explosion of 10 billion hydrogen bombs every second. Only a tiny fraction of this energy reaches us, but that amount is more than enough to support the expansive ecosystems that cover almost the entire surface of the earth. How the sun produces such remarkable amounts of energy was not understood until Albert Einstein derived his theory on the interrelationship of mass and energy: $E = mc^2$, where E stands for energy, m is mass, and c^2 is the speed of light. The vital principle revealed in this equation is that mass and energy can be interconverted.

The current theory is that extreme pressure in the sun's core, about one billion times stronger than that of the earth's atmosphere, forces atomic nuclei close together and speeds up their movement so that they collide and join together—a process termed *fusion*. The outcome of this thermonuclear reaction is a new fused nucleus that has slightly less mass than the starting nuclei. The difference in mass between the starting material and the product is released as pure energy.

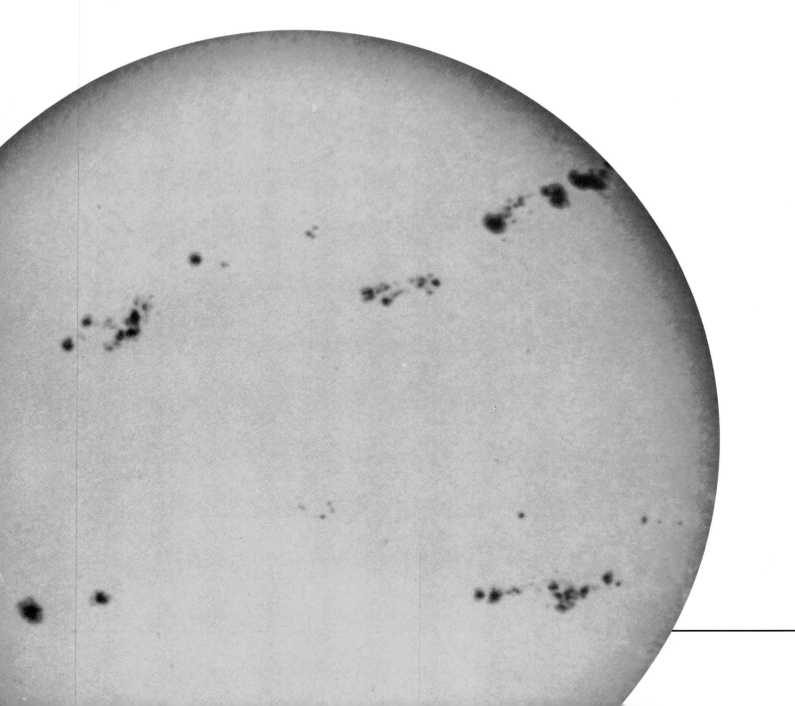

The main reaction in the sun's core is the conversion of hydrogen nuclei into helium. Every second, about 657 tons (591 metric tons) of hydrogen are changed into about 652.5 tons (587 metric tons) of helium. The difference—4.5 tons (4 metric tons)—is released as various forms of radiation. A small amount of mass altered in this way converts into a large amount of energy (remember that the speed of light, in the above equation, is a very large number). It is estimated that 2.2 pounds (one kg) of matter is equivalent to 25 billion kilowatt-hours of energy, which is the amount a large country uses in a few months. Thus the 4.5 tons (4 metric tons) of mass converted directly into solar radiation every second is a remarkably powerful outburst. This process uses up the sun's matter, causing it to continuously reduce in size. But the proportion of mass lost is insignificant compared to the sun's total mass: It is estimated that our sun will continue to burn for another several billion years.

The extremely high temperature of the sun's interior—approximately 27 million°F (15 million°C) in its core—is hot

Figure 7
REGIONS OF THE SUN: The middle region is called the *central core,* **which is surrounded by a** *zone of radiation.* **Next is the** *photosphere,* **followed by the** *chromosphere,* **and the turbulent outer layer is the** *corona.*

enough to melt and vaporize any substance. This means that despite the extreme interior pressure, the sun is made up totally of gases. The large central core is surrounded by a somewhat cooler layer called the *zone of radiation* (Figure 7). Outside this region is a thin layer known as the photosphere, so named because bombardment of this area sends out radiation in the visible light spectrum. The temperature of the photosphere is a relatively cool 11,000°F (6,000°C). Next is the chromosphere, which gives off weak red light. The outermost layer is the corona, a volatile region of diffuse gases in constant flux, with an average temperature of about 3.6 million°F (2 million°C)—much hotter than the adjacent layers. This may result from intense shock waves emanating from the photosphere, which superheat the corona's less dense gaseous material.

Sunspots are irregular blotches that appear on the surface of the photosphere. They appear to be darker because they are relatively cool, about 3,600°F (2,000°C) cooler than the surrounding gases. They range in size from 500 miles (800 km) in diameter up to 50,000 miles (80,000 km) across and last anywhere from a few days to several months.

The intriguing aspect of sunspots is that they are periodic. They arise, usually in pairs, at about 35 degrees latitude north and south of the sun's equator. With time, more spots appear, closer and closer to the equator, until at the cycle's peak many dark patches are seen across the surface. The spots then begin to recede, so that by cycle's end only a few spots near the equator remain. The average time for this solar cycle is eleven years.

Sunspots are associated with magnetic fields. The charged, swirling gases of the sun's exterior have magnetic character-istics. As these gases move, the magnetic lines of force also change. The paired nature of sunspots suggests they may be the positive and negative poles of a transitory magnetic field. The strong interaction between charged gases on the surface and these poles may block off the hottest gases, resulting in a localized cooling effect. Thus sunspots are most likely the product of magnetic disturbances that migrate over the photosphere in a rhythmic fashion.

An interesting recent discovery is that the sun's own magnetic field switches polarity regularly at the beginning of every solar cycle. This means that the north and south magnetic poles reverse approximately every eleven years, coinciding with sunspot activity. This finding is a further link between sunspots and solar magnetic activity, although the exact mechanism for sunspot formation remains to be defined.

Sunspots are thought to be the cause of other distortions of the sun's surface called *prominences*. These are massive plumes of hot gas that stream between spots, probably a reaction to the magnetic forces at work in these regions. Particularly strong prominences can break off into *solar flares*, hurling tons of superheated gases far out into space. Prominences and flares are best observed during a solar eclipse, when the moon blocks out all but the sun's corona, revealing the violent and dynamic atmosphere raging on our neighboring star.

Intense solar upheavals can result in large-scale magnetic disturbances on our own planet. On occasion these magnetic storms are severe enough to interrupt radio and television transmissions, as well as other types of electrical activities. Even a compass, which relies on the magnetic north pole to operate, can malfunction. Fortunately such disturbances are uncommon and temporary.

WHAT HAPPENS DURING AN ECLIPSE?

WITNESSING AN ECLIPSE OF THE SUN would probably be a frightening experience if you didn't understand what was happening. Imagine being outside on a bright clear day when suddenly the sky begins to grow dark, and light continues to fade until the sun itself becomes completely screened out behind a blackened circle. It's no wonder ancient civilizations ascribed supernatural importance to such events. Today we know how and why eclipses are formed and can even predict accurately when and where they will occur. We also know that they pass quickly without consequence, so a chance to observe one should not be passed up—even if it is a little scary.

As the earth and moon travel around the sun, they form shadows extending out into space. An eclipse occurs when the earth passes through the moon's shadow—a *solar eclipse*—or the moon travels through the earth's shadow—a *lunar eclipse*. The alignments that produce these phenomena are diagrammed in Figure 9 on the following page.

Eclipses are possible because the moon orbits the earth on approximately the same plane as the earth orbits the sun. If these orbits were exactly parallel, solar and lunar eclipses would take place regularly every month. But the moon's orbit is slightly tilted—about 5 degrees—in relation to the earth's orbit (Figure 8). This means that most of the time when the three bodies are aligned, the moon and earth are above or below each other, precluding an eclipse, because their shadows don't contact the other's surface.

The two points at which the lunar and earth orbits do cross are called *nodes*. A necessary condition for an eclipse, then, is that the moon must be positioned at a node precisely when all three spheres are in line. Since the moon occupies this position only twice a month, the occasion when this event coincides with precise alignment by all three celestial bodies is infrequent.

Knowing all the criteria necessary for an eclipse, it is possible to calculate the frequency of these events. There must be at least two solar eclipses a year. The maximum number of eclipses per year is seven: either five solar and two lunar, or four solar and three lunar.

A total solar eclipse occurs when the moon's *umbra*, the cone-shaped inner shadow completely blocked off from sunlight, falls on the earth. On the average, this happens only once every 360 years in any particular location. The maximum coverage for a total eclipse is an area 167 miles (267 km) in width, and it persists for only about seven and a half minutes. Solar eclipses are this brief and restricted because only the tip of the moon's umbra ever reaches the earth. The area of the earth's surface under a solar eclipse changes rapidly as the moon's shadow sweeps across the earth's surface. In 1973, a Concorde jet was able to stay under a total eclipse for seventy-four minutes by flying in the shadow's path as it raced along.

By a remarkable coincidence, the moon appears, from our vantage point on earth, as almost exactly the same size as the

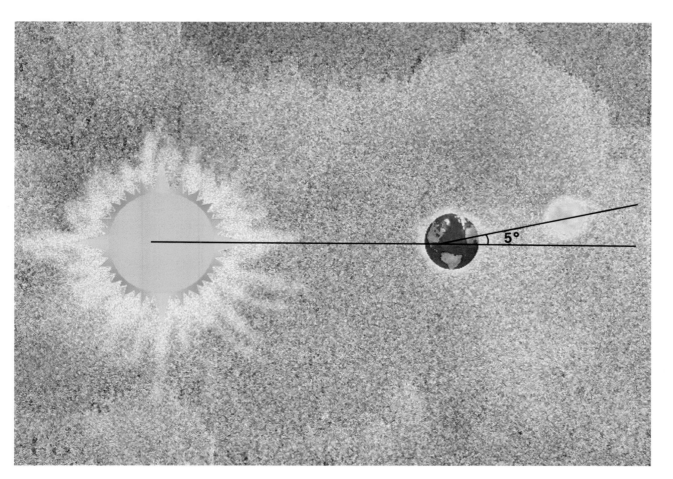

**Figure 8
PLANES OF ROTATION:** The plane of the lunar orbit is tilted about 5 degrees relative to the earth's orbit around the sun.

5°

sun. Thus, during a total eclipse, the moon fits precisely over the sun, blocking out all but its outer edge. This affords a brief glimpse of the sun's outer atmosphere, which is called the corona—a volatile gaseous halo that is otherwise invisible in the bright sky.

Sometimes the moon's shadow is aligned with the earth but doesn't quite reach the surface. This is because the earth and moon are not always the same distance apart. At its closest point, called *perigee,* the moon is 225,000 miles away (360,000 km), while at *apogee,* the two spheres are 240,000 miles (384,000 km) apart. If an eclipse occurs during apogee, the umbra does not extend far enough to reach the surface of the earth. The result is an *annular* eclipse (Figure 9), which is characterized by a bright ring of sunlight extending out over the moon's perimeter.

The next total solar eclipse to cross the continental United States will be in the year 2017. Canada must wait until the year 2024 for its next total eclipse. Although the area from which a total eclipse can be observed is relatively small, surrounding regions experience a *partial* eclipse, wherein some fraction of the sun is blocked off.

A lunar eclipse is a haunting and beautiful sight that occurs

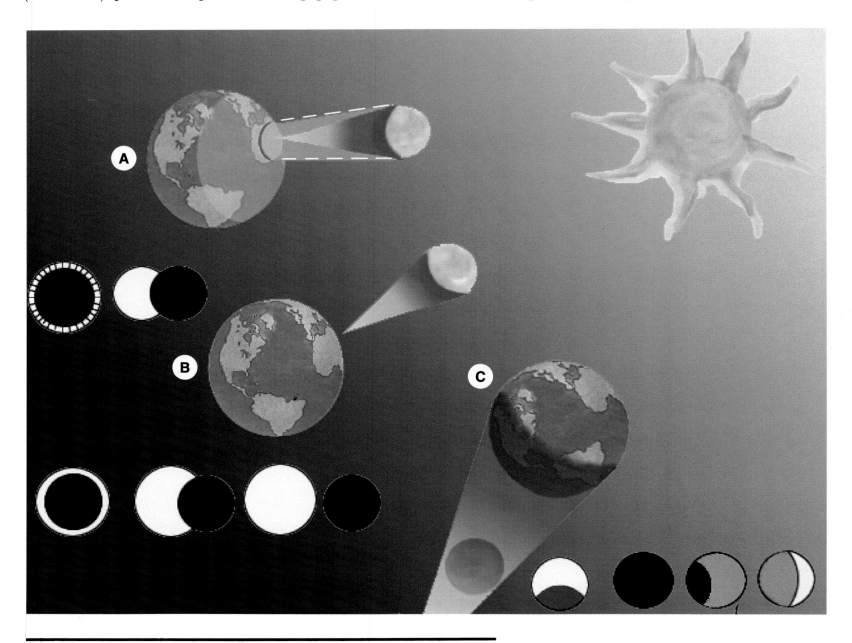

Figure 9
A. SOLAR ECLIPSE: This rare event occurs when the earth moves through the moon's shadow. Only a small portion of the earth's surface experiences a total eclipse, while a wider area is partially eclipsed.

B. ANNULAR ECLIPSE: This type of solar eclipse happens because the moon is sometimes farther away from the earth than usual, preventing the lunar shadow from reaching all the way to the earth's surface.

C. LUNAR ECLIPSE: A very rare phenomenon that occurs when the moon passes through the earth's shadow, a lunar eclipse covers the entire face of the moon.

even less frequently than the solar eclipse: There are only about seventy total lunar eclipses every century. Your chances of observing one from where you live, however, are much better than witnessing a total solar eclipse, since a lunar eclipse can be observed from a much larger area: nearly the entire dark half of the earth.

For a lunar eclipse to occur, the moon must enter the earth's umbra. The earth's *penumbra*—the outer part of its shadow— has little or no effect on the moon's appearance. A total eclipse can last for about one hour, while part of the moon can remain blocked out for up to two hours. During a total eclipse, the moon remains visible, though darkened. This is because the earth's atmosphere acts like a lens and bends sunlight into the shadow. The longer wavelengths of red light penetrate the atmosphere better than the short-wave blue light, giving the moon a strange reddish copper-colored glow.

Extensive cloud cover can block the dim light reflecting off an eclipsed moon to produce a very dark circular image. On rare occasions, the eclipsed moon is entirely out of sight. These extremely dark eclipses are due to major volcanic eruptions that fill the air with dust, obliterating any light directed back toward the earth from the eclipsed moon.

During a total solar eclipse, right, the moon blocks out the sun almost completely, leaving only the outer-most edges visible. The diagram below shows the blockage of the sun's light on a small portion of the earth's surface during a total solar eclipse.

© Michael Francis/The Wildlife Collection

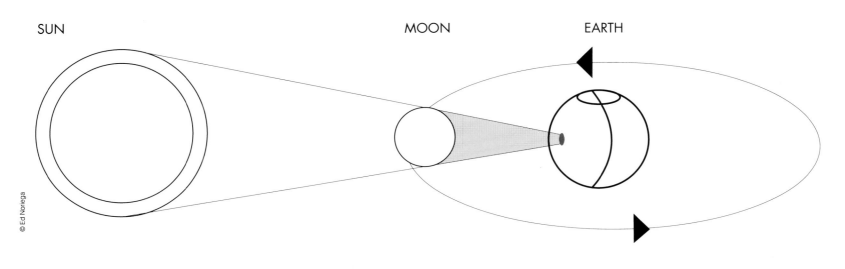

SUN   MOON   EARTH

© Ed Noriega

WHY DOES THE MOON WAX AND WANE?

OUR MOON IS CLASSIFIED AS A *satellite:* a celestial body that revolves around a planet. Because of its large size and close proximity, the moon has several important effects on the earth. This arrangement also makes it easy for the moon to be studied with even simple telescopes. In the modern era, man has visited the moon and examined it first hand, bringing back detailed information about the composition of this close neighbor. Together these methods have taught us a great deal about the structure and movement of our moon and also about satellites in general.

Compared to our warm and temperate planet, the moon is a very desolate and harsh world. Its surface is covered with craters, some nearly 800 miles (1,280 km) wide, created by meteor impacts long ago. There is no atmosphere on the moon and no trace of water; in fact, there are no volatile compounds of any kind. Analysis of moon rocks brought back by astronauts has revealed that the moon is enriched in elements that melt at high temperatures. Taken together, these features are evidence of the moon's violent history and provide a constant reminder of the tumultuous conditions under which our solar system was formed billions of years ago.

Locked in orbit around us, the moon makes one complete revolution around the earth every twenty-seven and one-third days. However, since the earth progresses in its own orbit around the sun during that time, it takes slightly more than two more days for the moon to reach its starting position relative to the earth (Figure 11). Thus the lunar cycle is designated as twenty-nine and one-half days.

Like the earth, the moon rotates on its axis as it orbits. It turns one complete revolution every twenty-seven and one-third days, exactly the same length of time as its orbit. This means that the same side of the moon's surface always faces the earth. The only way to see the back side is from outer space —a feat which has been accomplished in modern times by passing behind the moon in a spaceship.

This exact correlation between the moon's rotation and orbit is not coincidental. Scientists theorize that many millions of years ago, the moon actually rotated faster than it does now. But the earth's strong gravitational force exerted a braking action on the moon, gradually slowing down its rotation until one side was permanently locked in place facing our planet. The moon also exerts significant gravitational force on the earth and is very slowly decreasing its speed of rotation. Our days grow about one-thousandth of a second longer every 100 years.

When the moon is visible, it usually appears not as a full circle, but crescent shaped or as a half or partial circle. These *phases* of the moon occur in a predictable sequence over the

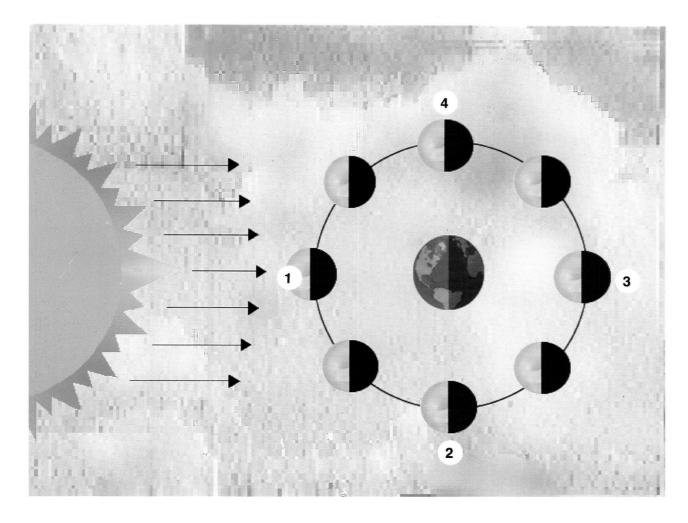

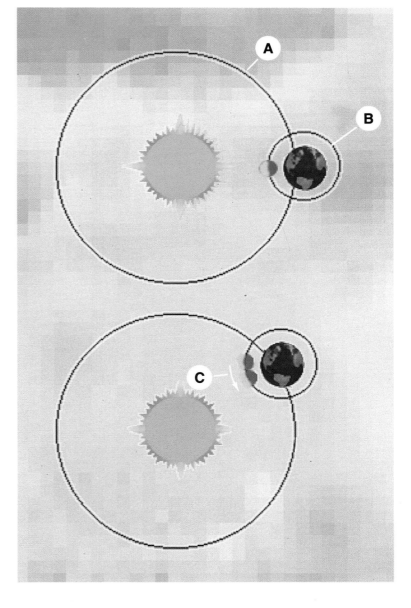

course of the lunar month as illustrated in Figure 10. At the beginning of the cycle when the moon is positioned between the earth and sun, the side of the moon visible to us receives no sunlight. This phase is designated the *new moon*. It appears only in the daytime sky and is difficult to see because the background sky is so light. The faint image we do see is a result of light reflected from the earth.

As the moon travels along its orbit and moves out from between the sun and earth, sunlight begins reaching part of the surface we can see from earth. This lighted surface appears as a thin sliver of light—a crescent—and initiates the *waxing* phase. The cycle progresses to the *first quarter*, when half the circle comes into view. This phase can be seen clearly during the daylight hours and is also visible for several hours after dark.

With time, more of the surface receives light until we see three-fourths of the moon's face. Finally the whole circle is lit up, the phase called the *full moon*, which can be observed only during the night. This marks the halfway point, when the moon's surface that faces us is also facing the sun. Thereafter the *waning* process begins, which exhibits the reverse pattern as the moon disappears in stages. More and more of the moon's surface fades into darkness until just half is visible (the *last quarter*), then a crescent, and then finally the new moon phase is reached after twenty-nine and a half days, and the cycle is positioned to start over again.

The moon phases should not be confused with eclipses, those rare occasions when the moon and earth actually throw shadows on each other. The waxing and waning moon is simply the result of sunlight illuminating only part of that aspect of the moon facing us.

WHAT CAUSES OCEAN TIDES?

IF YOU HAVE EVER BUILT sand castles on the seashore, you no doubt have experienced first hand the periodic rise and fall of the ocean's surface. As high tide approaches and the waves reach farther and farther up the beach, it becomes evident that makeshift barriers of any kind—seawalls, trenches, rocks, and driftwood—will not protect your masterpiece. At such moments, it is important to remember that tides cycle: The waves will eventually retreat, allowing construction of new and possibly even more dazzling architectural wonders.

Tides are caused by the moon's gravitational force on the earth. Gravity is the force of attraction that one physical entity exerts on another. The strength of that force is a function of the mass of the attracting object and its distance. The larger an object and the nearer it is, the stronger its gravitational force. Because the moon is large relative to the size of the earth, and because the moon is, on a planetary scale, fairly close to the earth, lunar gravity exerts strong effects on our planet.

One such effect is to pull the earth out of a strictly circular orbit around the sun. Although we tend to think of the moon as a satellite orbiting our planet, the fact is that the earth and moon rotate around each other. Because the earth is larger and more dense, the center of rotation for the two bodies is shifted toward the earth and lies at a point just inside the earth's circumference (Figure 12a). Thus as the earth circles the sun, it is pulled out of line and follows a zig-zag path as it travels through space (Figure 12b).

The sun also exerts gravitational attraction on the earth. Even though it is much larger than the moon, its further distance reduces its gravitational force to just less than half that of the moon's.

Large bodies of water are noticeably influenced by the gravitational pull of the moon. Because of its liquid state, water can change shape readily, adjusting to outside forces. The result is a localized bulge in the area of the ocean facing the moon and a compensatory bulge on the opposite side of the earth. Tides occur on the average every 12.4 hours—which is half the time required for the earth to complete one full rotation relative to the moon.

Figure 12
A. CENTER OF ROTATION: Because the mass of the earth is greater than the moon's, these two bodies rotate around a central point closest to the earth; in fact, this focal point is just under the earth's surface facing the moon.

B. EARTH'S ORBITAL WOBBLE: The moon's gravitational pull on the earth is strong enough to pull it out of a strictly circular path as it orbits the sun.

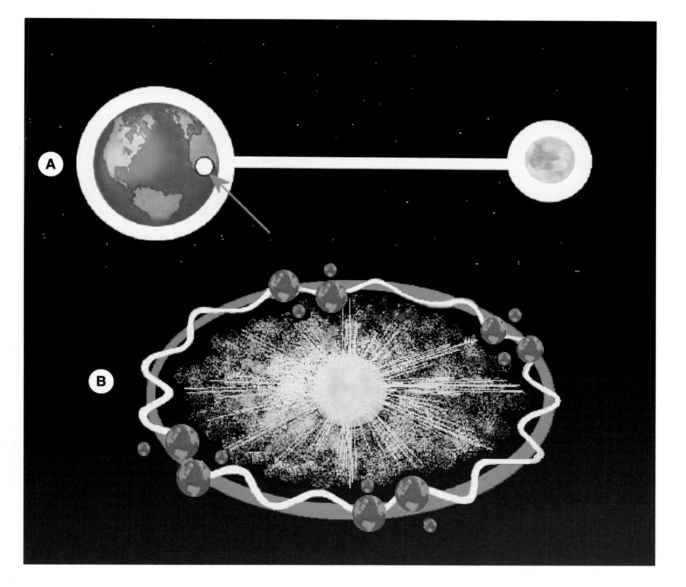

Figure 13
SPRING TIDES (right): Conditions for exceptionally strong tides occur when the moon and sun align to pull in the same direction against the earth's water surfaces.

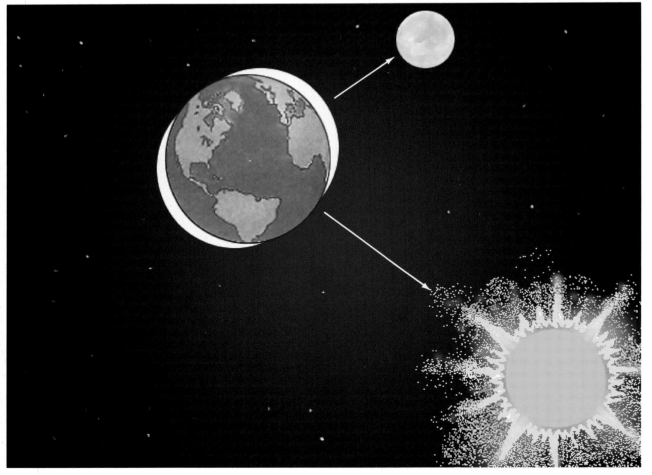

Figure 14
NEAP TIDES (left): Weak tides are produced when the moon and sun are positioned at a right angle with respect to the earth, partially canceling out gravitational forces on the oceans.

The main influence of the solar tide is to amplify or moderate the lunar tide. Since the solar tide cycle is slightly shorter than the lunar tide (every twelve hours instead of 12.4), these two series move in and out of synchrony every fourteen days. The strongest tides, called *spring tides,* occur when the sun and moon are so aligned that they pull in the same direction (Figure 13), complementing each other's gravitational forces on the oceans. When the sun and moon lie perpendicular with respect to the earth, their gravities largely cancel each other out causing *neap tides* (Figure 14), which are smaller than normal. Because the positions of the earth, moon, and sun are variable, other intermediate tides between these two extremes also occur.

If the earth was covered by an even layer of water, tides would be almost too small to measure. In the open ocean, the bulge created by the moon's gravity is only a fraction of an inch (or centimeter) high. It is when these initial bulges move across the ocean and approach continents that significant changes in water levels occur. The shape and depth of the ocean bottom and the contour of coastal regions play important roles in the level tides achieve.

Another important factor that determines tidal strength is the size and shape of the water mass involved. Any enclosed or semi-enclosed body of water exhibits a characteristic *period of oscillation.* This is the speed at which water, as a whole, slops forward and backward in its container. You may have propagated such oscillations yourself in a bathtub, where it takes only slight movement from side to side to set up a wave pattern that can push water high enough to splash out on the floor if you are not careful.

The length of time of these oscillations is determined by the size of the body of water. In general, the larger the water mass, the longer the oscillation cycle. When the natural oscillation period of a large water mass corresponds to the tidal cycle, the additive forces can produce drastic changes in water level. The Bay of Fundy on the shore of New Brunswick, Canada, has a period of oscillation that corresponds very closely to the tidal cycle of approximately twelve hours. High tide can raise the water level as much as fifty feet (15 m) and low tide nearly drains the entire bay. The Mediterranean Sea, on the other hand, has a narrow tidal range, because its natural oscillation period does not correlate with the tidal cycle.

Most coastal regions situated along oceans experience regular tidal activity every twelve and a half hours—but there are exceptions. Some points on the Gulf of Mexico have just one high and low tide each day instead of two. The east side of the Panama Canal has just one small tide each day, while the west side has two a day with a magnitude up to fifteen times greater than those of the other side. What causes the pattern of tides for a particular area can involve many separate factors, making it a complicated event. But routine observation and study can reveal predictable patterns of tidal activity for any location.

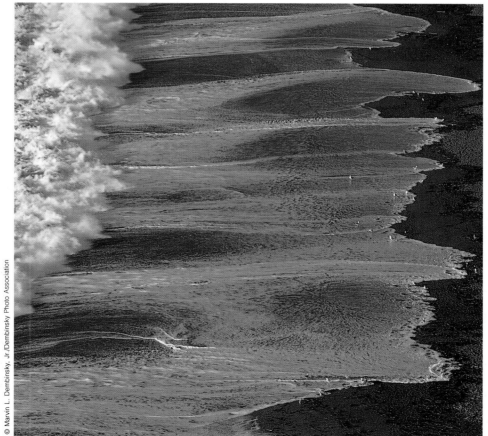

© Marvin L. Dembinsky, Jr./Dembinsky Photo Association

WHY DO COMETS PASS NEAR THE EARTH?

ONE OF THE MOST EXOTIC spectacles we can observe from the earth is the visitation of comets. These celestial intruders rocket into our solar system at high speed, spilling a trail of debris along their way, then exit back out into deep space. We tend to view our world and the space around us as a stable, isolated place. Comets are startling reminders that we are part of a larger, dynamic universe.

Where comets come from is uncertain, since telescopes cannot detect them until they are already within our solar system. Currently, the best guess is that a conglomeration of trillions of comets is positioned far outside the solar system. This *Oort Cloud* (named after the astronomer Jan Oort) is thought to circle the sun in an extremely distant orbit—so far out that it passes near other stars.

Several hypotheses have been put forth to explain the origin of the Oort Cloud. One idea suggests that a former planet within our solar system fragmented, throwing debris in all directions. Some larger pieces migrated toward Jupiter, where they became trapped in orbit to become moons, while smaller bits remained in orbit around the sun to form asteroid belts. But the bulk of this material drifted far out into space where it took up a distant orbit and remains as a diffuse gathering of planetary remnants. Another proposal is that comets are chunks of material that were never incorporated into planets or moons when our solar system was formed billions of years ago. These leftover materials eventually drifted away into deep space where gravitational attraction drew them into an extremely wide orbit around the sun.

As the Oort Cloud travels through space, it passes close enough to stars to be affected by them. Gravity from nearby stars can bend a comet's orbit, sending it off on a different course. Also, comets would be expected to randomly bump one another on occasion or be struck by smaller debris. Even minute deviations in a comet's direction of travel can send it on a new path that eventually intersects our solar system.

More than 600 comets have been identified to date, and a new comet is discovered about every other month on the average. Comets visible to the naked eye appear about once every two or three years, although most of these are not spectacular. Most comets have very long periods of revolution —100 years or more—while some return more frequently. Encke's comet, which has the shortest period, returns every three and one-third years. Halley's comet, the most well known of all, orbits through our solar system every seventy-six years.

The shape of cometary orbits is usually elliptical as shown in Figure 15. This is because the sun's strong gravitational force bends the comet's direction as it passes nearby, pulling it into a sharper angle as it bends around the sun. Once around the sun, the orbital path straightens out again as it escapes solar influence and heads away into deep space. Also, cometary orbits are usually tilted in relation to the orbital plane in which the planets of our solar system, except for Pluto, rotate (Figure 15).

The most distinguishing feature of a comet is the luminous tail that extends from the head far out into space. This bright stream, which can be millions of miles (or kilometers) long, consists of gases and debris trailing away from the main head. One might guess that this tail forms when part of the comet's exterior rubs off as the core plummets through our solar system at high speed. But friction cannot be the cause because outer space is a vacuum; there is no matter to create friction to tear at a comet's surface. In addition, the tail does not extend along behind the comet's direction of travel like a kite tail, but is actually perpendicular relative to the comet's orbit as it passes near the sun (Figure 15).

A clue to what produces the tail is the fact that it always points directly away from the sun. This implicates the solar winds, emanating outward from the sun, as the force that generates the tail. The high-speed particles within the solar winds dislodge part of the comet, carrying this material directly away from the sun to form the glowing tail. This hypothesis is strengthened by the observation that comets exhibit these streams only when they are in the vicinity of the sun.

A simple but apt description of comets is that they are "big dirty snowballs." The size of the central core or *head* ranges between one and ten miles (1.6 and 16 km) across and is composed of carbon compounds and various metals. Outside this core is a layer of ice, which partially vaporizes when it nears the sun to form the glowing halo and tail. The structure of the comet is intrinsically unstable and can lead to fragmentation. There is record of at least one such event, Beila's comet, which split apart and then disintegrated in the 1850s.

The sun is not the only sphere around which comets revolve. The larger outer planets such as Jupiter and Saturn sponsor dozens of cometary visits. Although most observed comets eventually return, some do not, evidently rerouted into different regions of the galaxy or dispersed into small remnants by fragmentation.

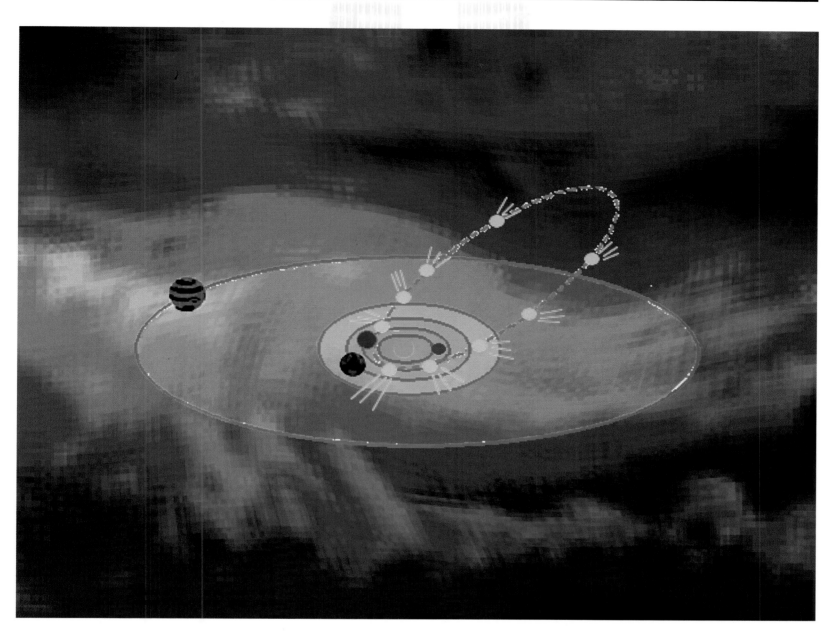

© Paul Ambrose/FPG International

Figure 15
COMETARY ORBITS
(above): Typically,
comets follow elliptical
paths rather than
circular ones and have
orbits that are tilted
relative to planets of
the solar system.

Set against the starry
night background, a
comet, left, stands out,
distinguished by its
bright flowing tail.

WHAT IS A SHOOTING STAR?

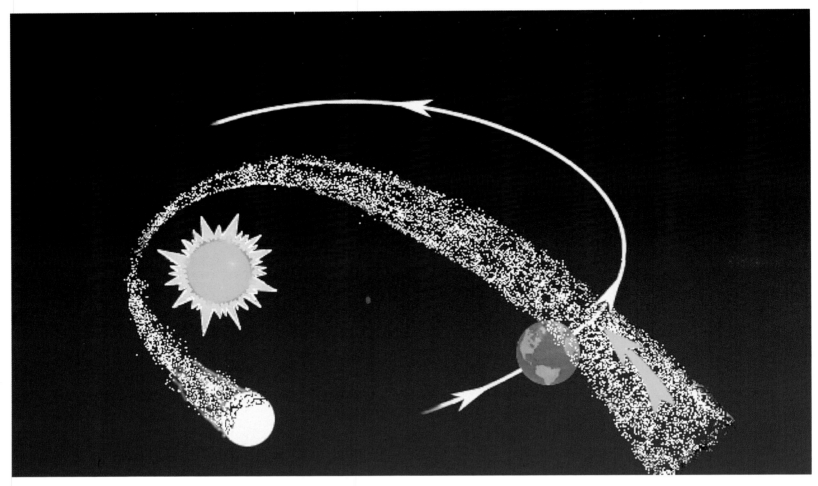

Figure 16
METEOR SHOWERS
(above): Heavy meteor activity often corresponds to the earth's passing through the remnants of a comet's trail.

This huge crater near Flagstaff, Arizona, left, is stark evidence that a huge meteor struck the earth thousands of years ago.

© J. Messerschmidt/FPG International

WATCHING METEORS STREAK ACROSS the night sky is possible any time of the year as long as the sky is clear. If you are patient and stay alert, you will see a brief flash of light race across the black background and instantly fade away. Although some last two or three seconds, most of these meteors burn out after only a fraction of a second. Sometimes a reddish glow is noticeable, although most often they appear white.

Meteors are pieces of extraterrestrial matter that race toward the earth at very high speed—about fifty miles (80 km) per second. Most of them are very small, weighing less than an ounce (or a few grams), although some are much larger. It is estimated that billions of these particles fall toward earth every day. As these objects enter the atmosphere and encounter its gaseous material, a high degree of friction is produced. This friction raises the temperature of the meteor rapidly until it begins to vaporize, giving off a flash of brilliant light as it disintegrates.

Most of the time, meteors burn up far above the earth. Occasionally, however, they penetrate completely and hit the ground. Such pieces of space debris are given the name *meteorites* and can vary in size from barely visible pebbles to gigantic rocks weighing several tons. On the average, several meteorites of significant size hit the earth every day, although most of them fall into the sea or drop in remote places where they are unlikely to be found. The impact often buries a meteorite, which is another reason they are not easily discovered.

Very large meteors leave unmistakable evidence of their arrival. A crater in northern Arizona measuring 4,000 feet (1,200 m) across and over 100 feet (30 m) deep is striking evidence that an object weighing thousands of tons hit the earth some 25,000 years ago. There is evidence of a large meteor landing in Russia in 1908, the impact of which blew down forests for many miles around. Fortunately meteorites of this size cross the earth's path very infrequently.

Although our world is constantly bombarded by cosmic debris, some nights bring exceptionally heavy meteor activity. On a few occasions, several thousand meteors have been spotted in a single night. Such meteor showers occur on a regular basis—usually once each year. The dates of the most significant of these annual displays are listed below.

Meteor swarms take place on these dates—and several nights before and after—because they coincide with the time when the earth passes through asteroid belts. These are areas of space where fragments and debris have accumulated, usually left over by a passing comet as diagrammed in Figure 16. In fact, most of the meteor showers listed occur when the earth travels across a comet's trail. For example, the Eta Aquarids occur when the earth moves through one point in the orbit of Halley's comet, and the Orionids coincide with the earth crossing another point in this same comet's path about five and a half months later.

An interesting feature of meteor showers is that activity increases through the course of the night. The number of sightings starts out lower in the evening and is nearly doubled toward morning. This is explained by the earth's movement and rotation. In the evening, your location is toward the back of the earth relative to its direction of orbit around the sun. This means that meteors must "catch up" with the earth in order to enter its atmosphere and fewer of them approach your location. Near morning, however, your position is now close to the front of the earth, which is plunging through the asteroid field. Thus an increased number of meteors are observed as the earth "chases down" more flying debris.

SHOWER	PEAK ACTIVITY	SIGHTINGS PER HOUR (average)
Quarantids	Jan. 3	30
Lyrids	Apr. 21	8
Eta Aquarids	May 4	10
Delta Aquarids	Jul. 30	15
Perseids	Aug. 12	40
Orionids	Oct. 21	15
Taurids	Nov. 4	8
Leonids	Nov. 16	6
Geminids	Dec. 13	50

WHY DO STARS TWINKLE?

FROM THE BEGINNING OF RECORDED history, people have been fascinated by the thousands of gleaming lights sprinkled across the nighttime sky. Studying the apparent movements of the stars revealed to early astronomers the rotation and orbit of our own planet as well as information about the dynamics of our solar system and points beyond. Today many people enjoy gazing into the heavens and learning about the patterns and positions of stars and discovering what stars tell us about our universe as a whole. From our planet, we can see about 6,000 stars with the naked eye. They vary in color, size, and brilliance.

We are close enough to one particular star—the sun—to know many details about what these celestial bodies are made of and how they function. A star consists of gases and other substances that compress together under the force of gravity. The pressure at the core of a forming star is sufficiently intense to initiate nuclear reactions that begin generating energy. During this process, matter is converted to energy, releasing large quantities of heat and light. Since part of a star's matter is used up in such reactions, all stars have a limited existence and will eventually burn out. Relative to our perception of time, however, stars have very long lives, measured in billions of years.

There are three major types of stars that can be seen from earth. Those with the greatest mass are categorized as *blue* or *white stars*. Gravity exerted by their enormous mass puts extreme pressure on the core of these stars, raising the internal temperature well above 27 million°F (15 million°C). The surface temperature of one such blue star, Sirius, is calculated to be nearly 20,000°F (11,000°C). These conditions sponsor a type of fusion termed the *carbon cycle*, in which traces of carbon are fused with other particles and then recycled again and again as energy is given off. A blue or white star is the hottest type of star, and thus is consumed rapidly and has a relatively short life span.

Yellow or *orange stars* are of intermediate size and are cooler. Our sun, with a surface temperature of about 11,000°F (6,000°C), fits in this category. The major reaction in the core of these stars is a fusion process that converts hydrogen to helium, with concurrent loss of mass and generation of radiant energy.

The third group are *orange* to *red stars*, which have masses between one tenth and one third that of the earth. They are named *red dwarfs* and have very long lives because they decay relatively slowly and at lower temperatures. A dwarf with about half the sun's mass can last 200 billion years, compared to the sun's expected life span of 10 billion years.

© FPG International

As a star uses up its mass and its nuclear furnace wanes, its total mass is the main factor that determines how it extinguishes. The smaller red dwarfs fade out quietly, dimming and contracting into a ball of helium called a *black dwarf*.

The end of larger stars is often more spectacular. As the core of these stars is spent, the inert helium by-product is sufficiently massive to be compressed under its own weight. This compaction eventually generates enough heat to ignite surrounding hydrogen gas, which expands and makes the star much larger. This pressurizes the core, producing even higher temperatures and expanding the hydrogen shell further until the star reaches the class of a *supergiant*. At this point, one of two dramatic events will occur. Moderately sized supergiants continue to heat up until they reach a critical point and explode. This is called a *supernova*, which sprays stellar debris over billions of miles of space, some of which will be recycled into new stars. If the supergiant is massive enough, it will collapse in upon itself as it runs out of energy, forming a *black hole*—a heavy core of matter so dense even light cannot escape its gravitational pull.

This violent life cycle of the stars seems far removed from the peaceful, glimmering scene we observe on a clear night, because even the nearest stars are positioned at an incredible distance from earth. Our nearest neighbor, Alpha Centauri, is nearly 25 trillion miles (40 trillion km) away. It is no wonder incoming light from such a distance is reduced to a faint twinkle.

The explanation for a star's twinkle is fairly simple. When a star's radiance approaches the earth, it encounters the atmosphere, which is composed of various molecular gases. This material is not stationary; layers of air tend to roll and swirl, even on a calm night. Because incoming starlight is very weak, small disturbances in the air bend and distort the beam, making the stars appear to twinkle on and off.

© FPG International

WHY IS THE NORTH STAR ALWAYS NORTH?

HEAVENLY CONSTELLATIONS HAVE been studied and mapped in such detail that virtually every visible star has been grouped into some formation. Greek astronomers were the first to systematically label and categorize the stars, and many of these designations are still used today, although most are known by other names as well. Some constellations are quite easy to locate and identify, such as Ursa Major (the Big Dipper), which resides in the northern sky.

More than half of the stars that surround us are invisible during any particular twenty-four-hour period. Those below the horizon are blocked from our view, and those near the horizon are often obscured by the sun's strong light as it sets and rises. But over the course of the year, we do get a chance to see different constellations. This is because we always view those stars facing the side of the earth away from the sun, which changes as the earth travels in its orbit around the sun.

Although different constellations are visible during various seasons, the positions of the stars are relatively fixed in space compared to earth. They are so far away from the earth that even our change in position as the earth journeys around the sun—a trip of 600 million miles (960 million km)—does not significantly alter our position in relation to them.

Watching the stars can be interesting and fun, but can serve a more practical function as well. Through the ages, navigators have relied on the position of certain stars to guide their path. In the northern hemisphere, one of the most important constellations for such purposes is Ursa Minor (the Little Dipper). This cluster includes Polaris—the North Star—which occupies a unique position in relation to the earth.

From most locations on the earth, the stars appear to journey from east to west across the night sky, due to the earth's counterclockwise rotation (see Figure 18 on page 42). At the equator, stars appear on the eastern horizon and track in nearly straight lines toward the west. But at points above the equator, the course stars travel is curved, inscribing circles around one star that doesn't move at all: Polaris. This is because Polaris sits almost directly over the north pole, the center point around which the earth rotates.

Polaris is designated the North Star because a line drawn straight through the earth's rotational axis out into space would pass less than one degree from this star. This line is called the *celestial north pole* (Figure 18). Since the North Star never sets and stays motionless in the night sky, it is a reliable guidepost for determining position and direction at night.

Although Polaris has been the star nearest the celestial north pole for centuries, it has not always been so. When the Egyptians built pyramids in 2700 B.C., they aligned them with Alpha Draconis, the star nearest true celestial north at that time. This deviation is attributed to a phenomenon called *processional motion*. This kind of motion is similar to what happens to a spinning top when the top of the toy wobbles and inscribes small circles in the air (Figure 17a, left). Our rotating planet exhibits this type of motion, which tilts its axis to point at different stars over time. The earth's processional movement is much slower than a top's though: It takes almost 26,000 years to complete one wobble. This motion is yet another way in which the gravitational forces of the sun and moon affect the earth.

Processional motion will eventually move the earth's celestial north pole away from Polaris. Figure 17b, above, shows that in the year 14,000 A.D., a very bright star, Vega, will be in position to reside as this world's north star.

Figures 17a and 17b ROTATIONAL WOBBLE: Just as a spinning top moves in a slow wobble as it spins, left (Figure 17a), the earth also does not rotate in a perfectly straight manner. This extremely slow wobble will eventually change what star lies directly over the north pole, above (Figure 17b): The current north star, Polaris (A), will be replaced in about 12,000 years by another star, Vega (B).

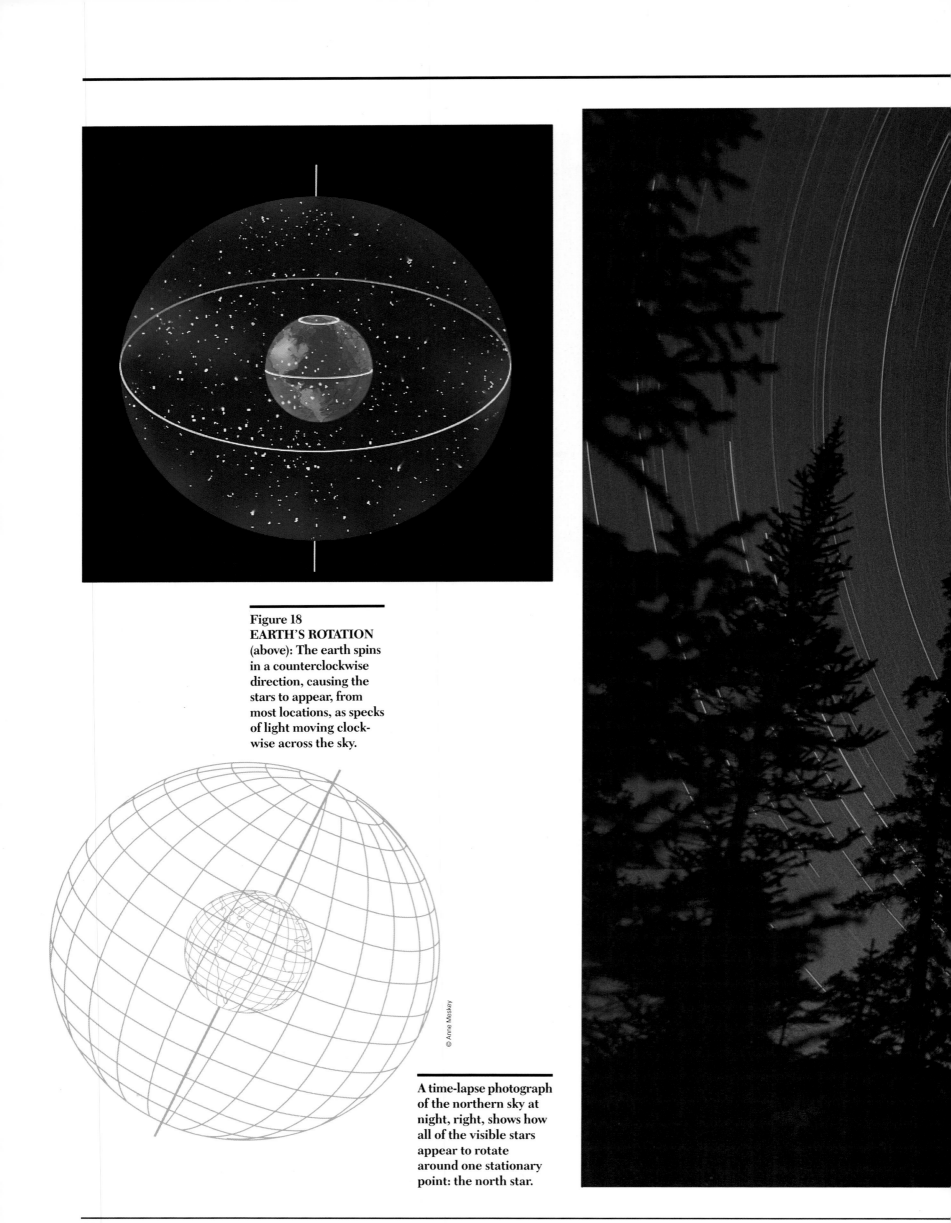

Figure 18
EARTH'S ROTATION
(above): The earth spins
in a counterclockwise
direction, causing the
stars to appear, from
most locations, as specks
of light moving clock-
wise across the sky.

© Anne Meskey

A time-lapse photograph
of the northern sky at
night, right, shows how
all of the visible stars
appear to rotate
around one stationary
point: the north star.

WEATHER
AND
CLIMATE

WHY DO THE SEASONS CHANGE?

© John Shaw/Tom Stack & Associates

© Willard Clay/Dembinsky Photo Association

WE HAVE ALREADY CONSIDERED SEVERAL of the phenomena that occur because of the earth's various types of motion. We experience such a smooth ride on our planet that these movements are not obvious—a fact that led many early observers to conclude that our world was motionless in space. They assumed that the sun, moon, and stars all moved around us and decided that our planet was the center of the universe and thus an extraordinarily important world.

Today we know that the earth simultaneously spins, wobbles, zigzags, and orbits the sun while it is also moving with the sun in orbit around the center of our galaxy. We are indeed going every which way at once, even when we are just standing still. So much for our status as the center of all things.

The earth completes one orbit around the sun in a little over 365 days. During that time, most locations on the globe experience changes in the average daily temperature that

dramatically alter the appearance of our surrounding environment. Based on these recurring and predictable cycles, the year is divided into summer, spring, autumn, and winter.

Seasons occur because the earth's axis of rotation is tilted relative to the plane of its orbit around the sun. All of the planets in our solar system exhibit some degree of tilting or *inclination*. The earth's angle of inclination is twenty-three and a half degrees. This tilted orientation is maintained as the earth travels through space along its orbit, which means that various parts of the earth receive different amounts of sunlight during the year.

The north pole is maximally tilted toward the sun on June 21 or 22 (Figure 20). This marks the *summer solstice,* the longest day of the year in the northern hemisphere. At this time, the sun lies directly over the *Tropic of Cancer*—an imaginary line that inscribes the northernmost latitude at which the sun is

directly overhead at midday. At points north of the Tropic of Cancer, which includes the United States, the sun never quite achieves a strictly vertical path and always appears in the southern half of the sky at noon. In regions near the north pole, the sun doesn't set at all for the full twenty-four-hour period of this solstice, because the top of the earth is continuously pointed toward the sun.

As the earth proceeds along its orbit, the sun passes in a lower and lower arc across the sky of the northern hemisphere. On September 22 or 23, the *autumnal equinox* occurs, when the sun is positioned directly above the equator at midday. This marks the beginning of autumn. Three months later, on December 21 or 22, the *winter solstice* takes place, correlated with the halfway point along the earth's orbit. At this time, the sun's rays fall directly on the *Tropic of Capricorn*, the southern hemisphere's equivalent of the Tropic of Cancer. For locations

south of the equator, this is the longest day of the year, while areas close to the north pole are under almost total darkness for twenty-four hours.

On March 21 or 22, the equator is again positioned directly under the sun, a day called the *vernal equinox*, which marks the three-quarter point in the earth's journey. The cycle is completed three months later in June, when we once again experience the summer solstice and the earth begins another trip around the sun.

This pattern explains why the seasons are opposite one another in the northern and southern hemispheres. In Figure 20, it can be seen that the northern hemisphere receives the most sunlight when the southern hemisphere is minimally exposed. Thus cold winter months in the United States coincide with optimum beach weather in South America. Locations near the equator experience the least change in seasons, since they receive a fairly constant amount of sunlight every day of the year.

The change in seasons, then, can be attributed to increases or decreases in the length of time during which a particular location receives sunlight. Longer days allow increased exposure to solar radiation, which heats an area to a higher average temperature during the summer, while the shorter days of winter result in lower overall temperatures.

Another important factor that contributes to seasonal fluctuations in temperature is the *efficiency* of the sun's heating effect on the earth. In June when the northern hemisphere experiences its longest days, the sun achieves its most direct angle on this region. This means that sunlight must pass through less atmosphere to reach the ground, which results in less energy dissipation. The more direct angle also produces less reflection of incoming light, so that heat absorption by the earth's surface is maximized when the sun is more directly overhead (Figure 19).

The atmosphere itself amplifies the sun's heating capacity by a phenomenon called the *greenhouse effect*. The clear panels of a greenhouse allow sunlight to enter and warm the air inside and also form an enclosed structure that retains heat by sealing off the warmed interior from cooler air outside. In a similar manner, the atmosphere captures heat generated by the sun. When solar radiation reaches the earth, it is absorbed. This warms the ground which then transfers heat energy into the air, mostly in the form of infrared rays. These wavelengths are readily absorbed by the air, trapping the heat in the lower atmospheric layers. This helps maintain a constant, relatively warm average temperature at the earth's surface from day to day.

The greenhouse effect is currently an important issue because small changes in certain atmospheric gases, especially carbon dioxide, can significantly influence how much heat is captured at the earth's surface. Some scientific studies suggest that wide-scale pollution—which results in increased carbon dioxide in the air—is gradually warming global climates. If this continues, it will alter our environment in several ways, including extensive melting of the polar ice caps and raising the sea level. Thus the greenhouse effect provides us with a pressing reason to clean up our act and stop the pollution gripping our planet.

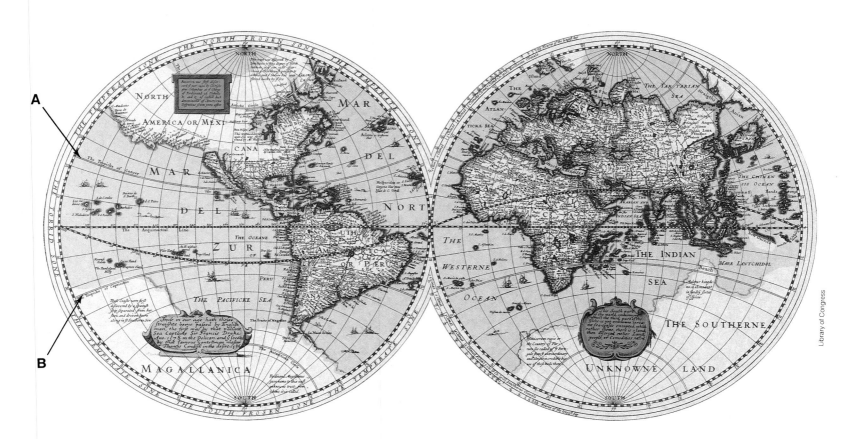

THE TROPICS OF CANCER AND CAPRICORN: When the sun lies directly over the Tropic of Cancer (A), the northern hemisphere experiences the longest day of the year. South of the equator, the longest day occurs when the sun is above the Tropic of Capricorn (B).

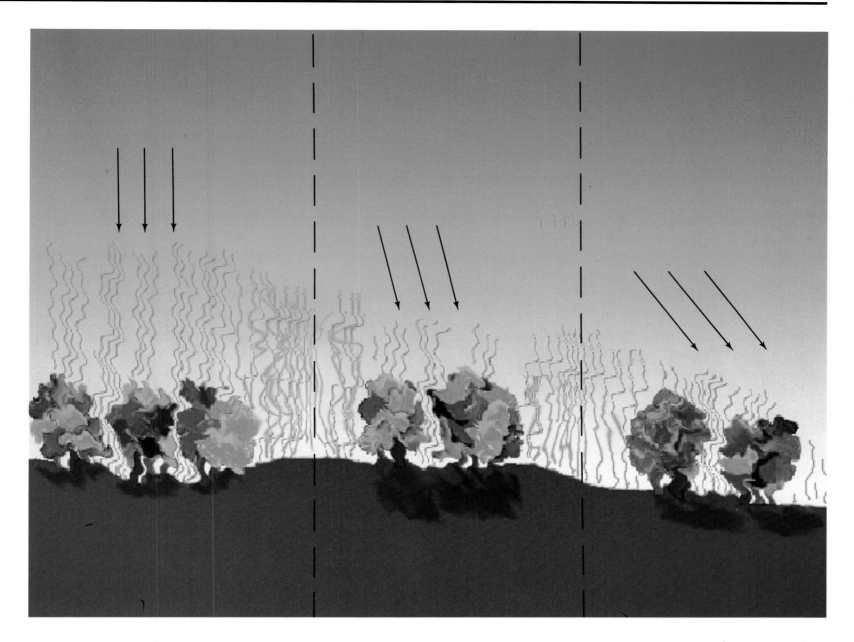

Figures 19 and 20
ANGLE OF THE SUN
(above, Figure 19):
Sunlight from directly
overhead heats the
earth's surface most
efficiently, while angled
solar radiation is not as
effective. **OPPOSITE
SEASONS IN THE
TWO HEMISPHERES**
(right, Figure 20):
A) Winter in the north-
ern hemisphere occurs
when that region is
tilted farthest from the

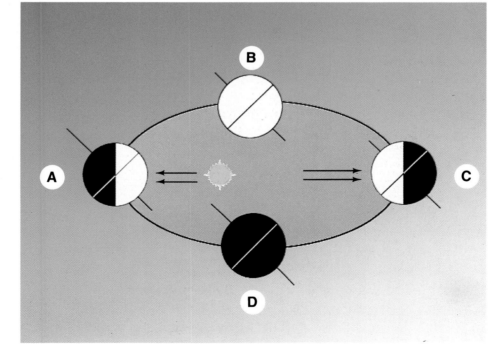

sun, the same time that
the southern hemi-
sphere is maximally
exposed; B) during the
fall, these two regions
have similar angles
to the sun and both
experience interme-
diate temperatures;
C) summer in the north
is matched by the cold-
est months in the south;
D) spring again posi-
tions both hemispheres
at similar angles to in-
coming solar radiation.

WHY DOES THE WIND BLOW?

Our atmosphere is often called an "ocean of air." This is a fitting description because the sky above us is not just empty space. It is composed of substances such as nitrogen, oxygen, carbon dioxide, and water—the same kinds of elements we are made of—with mass and weight and all the characteristic properties of physical matter. The difference is that in air the molecules are farther apart, floating in a gaseous phase in which the attraction between individual molecules is very weak.

The earth's gravity attracts the gaseous atmosphere just like all other matter, pulling it down against the surface. Despite its low density, the volume of air surrounding our planet is large enough to exert considerable force. At sea level, air pushes down at a weight of 14.7 pounds per square inch (2.6 kg per square centimeter) of surface area. This force is exerted equally in all directions, so that an average-size person has 44,000 pounds (20,000 kg) of pressure constantly pressing in on them. We don't notice this pressure because it is matched by an equal amount of pressure inside our bodies pushing outward.

Rapid changes in altitude, such as driving up into mountains or taking a plane ride, can make you aware of changes in air pressure. The popping sensation in your ears is caused by the pressure inside your head pushing air outward as your body adapts to the decreased air pressure at higher elevations. A sudden absence of air pressure would be fatal, which is the reason astronauts wear pressurized suits when venturing out into space where there is a total absence of air and hence the pressure is zero.

The phenomenon that convincingly displays the atmosphere's material composition is wind: the movement of an air mass in relation to the earth's surface. Feeling a breeze on your face or watching trees sway in a strong gust is proof that physical matter is moving through the invisible sky. What are the forces that cause the air to move?

Once again it is the sun that acts as the primary factor in generating this natural phenomenon. As solar radiation contacts the earth's surface and warms it, heat is transferred to the air by a process called *conduction*. This is a secondary transfer of energy by warmed objects and surfaces to surrounding gaseous molecules in the air. Sunlight can also warm the atmosphere before it reaches the ground. This process, called *radiation*, is a direct absorption of radiant energy by atmospheric gases. Energy from the sun does not energize all regions of the atmosphere evenly—the air next to the earth's surface is heated more efficiently than the region just above.

The temperature of an air mass determines its density. When molecules in the air absorb energy in the form of heat, they exhibit increased motion, which keeps them far apart from one another and decreases the overall density. As molecules lose energy, they pack together more tightly causing the density to increase. Because warmer air is less dense, it also exerts less pressure than cooler air. This means that warm air tends to rise, and it is this movement of unevenly heated masses of air, a phenomenon termed *convection*, that causes wind.

An area where warm air is rising is said to be under a *low pressure* system, since the air pressure in this region is less than normal. Conversely, a location where cooler air is flowing downward is a *high pressure* area, where the air pressure is elevated. The instrument used to measure these changes is called a *barometer*, which is why you hear the measurement of air density reported as a barometric pressure reading.

To understand how wind operates, let's consider the special case of how air flows in coastal areas. During the day, sunlight heats the air over the shore more efficiently than the air above the ocean. This is because the land surface absorbs heat efficiently and then warms adjacent air by conduction, while the constant movement of the ocean mixes the warming surface layer with cooler water below, distributing heat and keeping the surface cool. Also, water demonstrates a lower capacity for absorbing and releasing heat than solid land. This means water requires more heat energy to increase in temperature than land surfaces. In addition, water releases heat in the form of evaporation, which helps maintain its more constant temperature.

The warmer air above the land rises, creating a localized low pressure area. Cooler air over the adjacent ocean waters rushes in to replace the rising air above the shore, creating the constant "sea breeze" experienced along coastal regions (Figure 21).

At night, the land cools off rapidly while the water retains heat longer and thus maintains a fairly constant temperature. This means the coolest air is now above the land, a situation that reverses the direction of air flow and causes wind to sweep out toward the ocean. These patterns of cool ocean breezes during the day and warm winds from inland at night maintain relatively stable conditions along coastlines, which typically experience less daily fluctuation in temperature than other geographical regions.

On a global scale, winds are generated according to this same principle: movement of unevenly heated air masses. But the pattern and direction of the earth's wind currents take on a special "twist," so to speak, because our planet is in motion. As the earth rotates on its axis, the surface is in effect dragged through the ocean of air surrounding us. How this rotation influences global wind currents is the subject we will examine next.

Figure 21
OCEAN BREEZE
(above): Rising air
above land regions
causes cooler air over
oceans to flow inland,
creating wind.

WHAT CAUSES OCEAN CURRENTS?

THE WORLD'S OCEANS are not just motionless bodies of water. Within the seas, there are great "rivers" that constantly circulate in specific directions. Early explorers made use of ocean currents to sail all over the globe, and navigators on sea vessels today carry detailed charts of these currents.

The source of the ocean's currents was thought by some early scientists, including Galileo, an Italian physicist and astronomer, to be produced by the earth's rotational motion on large bodies of water. This turns out not to be the case: Although it is true that planetary movements do affect the direction of winds and thus play an indirect role, it is wind that is responsible for creating ocean currents. But there is no need to apologize for Galileo—he got an incredible number of very important principles right. If scientists don't make a few errors now and then, they just aren't trying hard enough.

The force of winds pushing across the surface of the ocean puts avenues of water in motion. Let's examine the forces that create the earth's wind patterns, and then we will consider how well ocean currents correlate with the prevailing air currents.

If the earth did not rotate and the sun revolved around us instead of the other way around, our wind currents would follow a very simple pattern. Since regions at the equator receive more radiation from the sun than other latitudes, air would continuously rise from this central area and spread both north and south high above the earth's surface. Cooler air at the poles would push down and flow along the ground toward the equator, and the wind would always blow south in the northern hemisphere and north in the southern hemisphere.

Our planet's rotation bends north and south flowing wind currents by sweeping the earth's surface under them. The principle that describes this phenomenon is called the *Coriolis effect*, after Gaspard Coriolis, the French mathematician who analyzed and reported it. To understand this effect, let's consider what would happen to an airplane that took off from the north pole and headed straight south toward New Orleans. During the time it takes to fly this distance, the revolving earth would move underneath the airplane, so that the flight would arrive in Los Angeles instead of the original destination. This is a factor aerial navigators take into account when charting courses going in north or south directions.

With these facts in mind, we can understand what causes the dominant wind currents on our planet that are illustrated in Figure 22. At the equator, the only significant atmospheric movement is heated air rising straight up. This produces only mild and occasional winds, which is why the equatorial belt is referred to as the *doldrums*. As warm air rises from the equator, it turns and spreads out in both directions. At about 30 degrees latitude, these air masses cool off and drop back toward the surface, creating high pressure belts in both hemispheres known as the *horse latitudes*, also characterized by light winds, since the major air movement is straight down.

As air falls back to earth in these regions, it splits and tracks both north and south. In the northern hemisphere, the portion folding back toward the equator is bent to the left by the Coriolis effect to form the *northeast trade winds* (winds are named according to the direction they blow *from*). Air flowing north from the upper horse latitudes is diverted to the right to form the *westerlies*. The Coriolis effect bends the air flow emerging from the southern horse latitudes in the opposite directions. Thus, air moving back toward the equator is moved to the left, forming the *southeast trade winds*, and the southern hemisphere's *westerlies* are bent to the right.

Low pressure regions over the poles cause cool air to flow south. These currents are directed to the left in the northern hemisphere to create the *polar easterlies*. At the south pole, these winds have the same name but are curved to the left. Between the polar easterlies and westerlies of both hemispheres, at a latitude of approximately 65 degrees, is another belt of low pressure, and here again there is another zone of calm air.

Knowing what causes the earth's wind systems, it is easy to understand the pattern of the ocean's major currents as shown in Figure 23. Even a quick inspection reveals how closely water movements follow the direction of air flow. An interesting feature of these currents is the direction in which they cycle in the northern and southern hemispheres. Those above the equator bend in a clockwise direction, while those below move in counterclockwise circles. It is the Coriolis effect, curving winds in various directions, that accounts for these opposite rotational patterns of ocean currents in the two hemispheres.

Figure 22
**MAJOR WIND
PATTERNS** (right):
A) polar easterlies
(northern hemisphere);
B) westerlies (north-
ern hemisphere);
C) northeast trade
winds; D) southeast
trade winds; E)
westerlies (southern
hemisphere); F) polar
easterlies (southern
hemisphere).

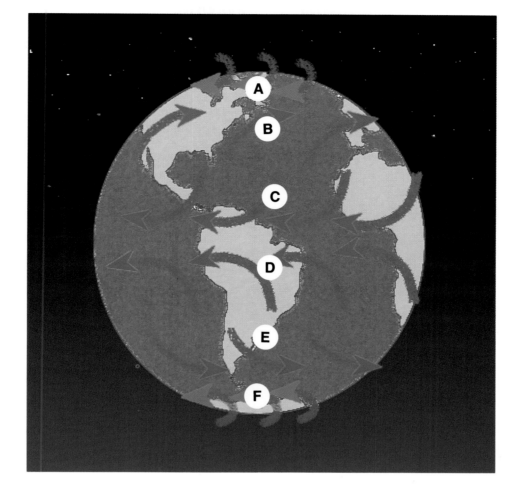

Figure 23
**OCEAN CURRENTS
OF THE WORLD**
(below): Major ocean
currents are shown as
lines, with direction
of flow indicated by
arrows. Note that in the
northern hemisphere
most currents bend
clockwise, while in the
southern hemisphere
the general trend is
counterclockwise.

HOW DOES A WAVE FORM?

IN ADDITION TO GENERATING CURRENTS in the oceans, wind has another important influence on bodies of water: the creation of waves. The force of air pushing against a liquid distorts the surface, setting the liquid in motion. Even a slight breeze contains sufficient energy to disturb an otherwise smooth surface of water. Once small ripples are started, air moving across the surface contacts the water at a more direct angle, pushing against the sides of waves, which increases their size even more.

The highest point of a wave is called the *crest,* and the low point between two crests is known as the *trough.* Important features of waves include their height—the distance from crest to trough—and their length—the distance between adjacent crests.

Casual observation of ocean waves can give the impression that they carry water forward along their path as they travel, but this is not the case. If you concentrate on some object floating in the water, you will see that it moves backward slightly as a wave approaches, is lifted up over the crest, and is pulled forward slightly as it lowers into the trough. The object has moved in a circular motion, not forward, ending up about where it started. This is exactly what happens to the water in a wave's path (Figure 24). It simply rotates in a circle as the wave passes, without significant lateral movement. Thus it is the wave itself that moves along the surface, not the water.

Constant wind flowing from one direction in the open sea can create groups of large waves that are all the same size and spaced evenly apart. These regular patterns are called *swells.*

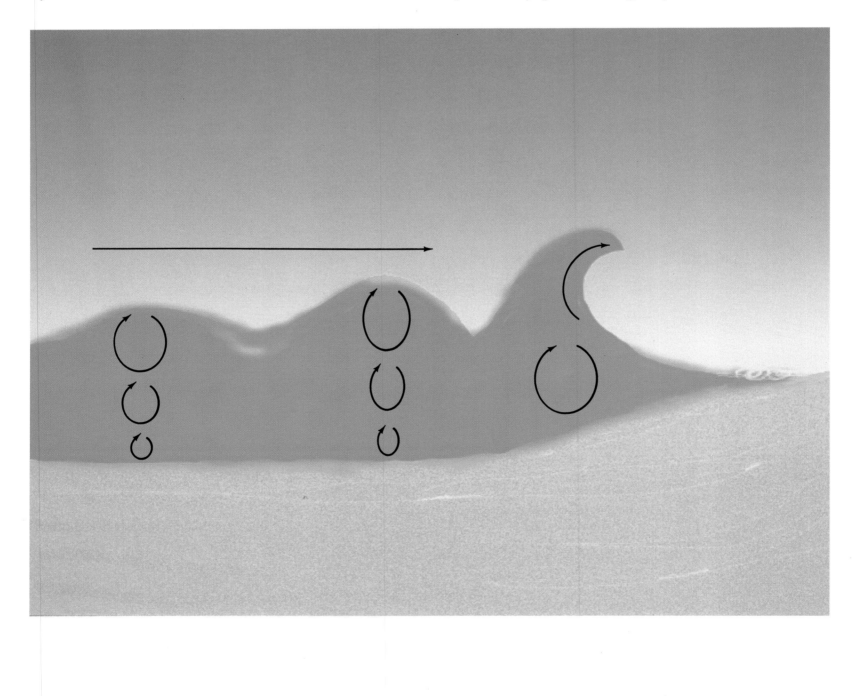

Ocean swells can travel thousands of miles (or kilometers) in open waters without being disrupted. As they approach land, the shallower ocean floor causes the wave shape of swells to change. The motion of water at the bottom of the wave is distorted by the underlying hard surface. This forces water upward in an elliptical pattern instead of a circular one, which increases the height of the crest. As the wave runs up onto the beach, the crest grows to such a height that it can no longer be supported and spills forward as a *breaker* (Figure 24).

In the open sea, swells can grow to enormous dimensions. During heavy storms, strong winds can whip waves to a height of 100 feet (30 m) or more. Despite their huge size, such waves are not usually dangerous to large ships, which move in a circular motion above the passing wave just as the water at the surface does. In severe conditions, strong blasts of wind blow the tops of these large waves over, forming *whitecaps*. These can be hazardous to a ship if it is positioned sideways when a whitecap hits.

The most powerful and dangerous waves of all, known as *tsunamis*, are produced by seismic events that shift the ocean floor. When earthquakes move the ground beneath a large water mass, the water above moves as well. This creates a large disturbance at the surface, which is transmitted outward in all directions. When tsunamis approach coastal regions, they build into gigantic waves with incredible power. For this reason, seismic activity in the Pacific Ocean region is carefully monitored. Detection of earthquakes under the ocean that may cause tsunamis is followed by warnings to coastal areas.

Figure 24
WAVE PRODUCTION (left): Initiated by the pressure of wind against the surface of water, waves are propagated by the rolling motion of the water beneath. As the depth of the ocean floor decreases as the beach approaches, this motion pushes the crest of a wave over into a breaker.

© Darrel R. Jones

WHY IS WATER WET?

SEVERAL OF THE NATURAL PHENOMENA presented so far, and many of those yet to be discussed, have something to do with water. No other compound figures so importantly in so many different ways on our planet. Water covers most of the earth's surface, is abundant in our atmosphere, flows beneath the solid ground, and is a vital component of all living systems. Within our solar system and the universe beyond, water is a rare substance; it is totally absent on most other planets.

Because of its central role in numerous terrestrial systems, let's examine the nature of water in some detail. An understanding of this compound's special chemistry will enrich our perspective of the other topics in this book. The mere sound of the word *chemistry* is enough to elicit groans from most readers and make them quickly skip ahead to the next section. But chemistry, like any field of science, is an organized set of principles that is really quite simple when taken one step at a time. So give this a try.

A water molecule consists of one oxygen *atom* combined with two hydrogen atoms. Atoms are the elemental building blocks of all matter and are the smallest units matter can be broken down to under normal conditions. Atoms consist of smaller units too: *protons, neutrons,* and *electrons.* Protons and neutrons are gathered in the center of an atom to form the *nucleus,* while electrons move around the nucleus in specific positions called *orbitals.* Protons carry a positive charge, and electrons are negatively charged, while neutrons are electrically neutral. The atom is held together by the force of the positively charged nucleus attracting the negatively charged electrons.

Atoms can combine into *molecules* by sharing their outer electrons to form chemical bonds that hold atoms together in a group. The water molecule—designated chemically as H_2O— is formed when two hydrogen atoms each share their single electron with two electrons of a single oxygen atom. Each pair of electrons, one from a hydrogen atom and one from the oxygen, form a single *covalent* bond, which is a strong attraction that holds the hydrogen nuclei close to the oxygen atom. But since oxygen starts with six electrons, there are now four electrons left over that do not bond. These four unshared electrons, which group into two pairs, give the water molecule unusual properties. To understand this, let's consider a more complete bonding arrangement in a different molecule.

Unlike oxygen, carbon atoms form molecular arrangements that use up all their outer electrons. Carbon can form four equal bonds with four hydrogen atoms to produce methane as drawn in Figure 25. The straight lines between atoms in this illustration represent covalent attachments—the two shared electrons that form the chemical bond. In three-dimensional space, the four hydrogen atoms in methane get as far away from each other as possible. This shapes the methane molecule into a *tetrahedron*, a geometric shape with four equal triangular sides. You can think of methane as being shaped like a camera tripod, with three poles flaring down to make legs and one pole up to hold the camera. The four hydrogen nuclei in methane carry a partial positive charge due to the proton at their center, while the carbon atom in the middle is partially negative from the shared electrons that are pulled in closer to the carbon. The symmetrical geometry of the methane structure distributes these partial charges evenly over the center of the molecule so that there is no net polarity—the positive and negative regions cancel each other out.

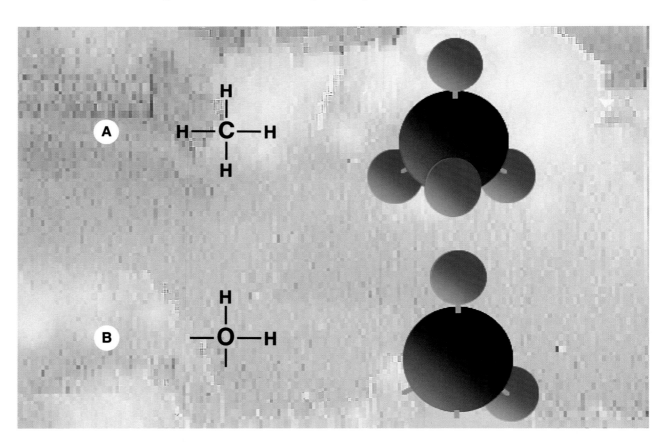

Figure 25
MOLECULAR STRUCTURE OF METHANE AND WATER: A) Methane forms a shape called a *tetrahedron* with four evenly spaced hydrogens surrounding a central carbon atom; B) water has only two hydrogens attached, giving it a nonsymmetric shape and unusual properties.

The water molecule displays a different structure. The two pairs of unshared electrons take up positions as far away from the two other electron pairs involved in bonds, giving the water molecule a tetrahedral conformation, but two of the four legs are just electrons, without bonded neighbors. This swings the two hydrogen atoms to one side of the oxygen, while the two pairs of unshared electrons occupy the other side.

What all this means is that water is a *polar* molecule. The two hydrogen nuclei give one side of the molecule a partial positive charge, while the unshared electrons give a partially negative charge to the other side. This polarity causes water molecules to attract one another: The negative end of one molecule associates with the positive end of another molecule. Thus, a body of water is *cohesive*. This cohesiveness is what makes water bead up on a smooth nonporous surface such as glass or metal as the individual molecules pull together into a clump.

This polarity along with a small size and symmetrical shape allow water molecules to pack together tightly and form a solid at a relatively high temperature. Most other liquids solidify at much lower temperatures, leaving water as the only substance that can exist in all three states within a relatively narrow temperature range.

Water is known as the "universal solvent" because it can dissolve a wide variety of substances. In fact one way that chemists categorize various substances is according to how well they dissolve in water. Again this property is a feature of the water molecule's physical characteristics. An example is how water dissolves granules of table salt, which is composed of sodium and chloride atoms linked together by covalent bonds. The negative oxygen atoms of water molecules associate with positive sodium ions, while positive hydrogens tie up negative chloride ions. This separates the two components of salt, keeping them away from each other in a solution.

In summary, water is a highly versatile compound with unique properties that sponsor many different kinds of important chemical interactions. In sections to follow, we will consider further how the special chemistry of water allows it to participate in many of the natural phenomena we observe on our planet.

HOW DOES DEW FORM?

WE NOTED EARLIER THAT the atmosphere contains a significant amount of water vapor. This gaseous form of H_2O contributes to the warming of the earth's surface by trapping sunlight in the lower regions of the atmosphere. Water vapor is also the source of life-sustaining rain that is delivered to land masses. Thus, the gaseous form of water plays a key part in the earth's water cycle.

The physical state of a body of water is determined by the energy level of the individual molecules within it. At temperatures below 32°F (0°C), H_2O molecules exhibit only limited movement and pack together tightly into solid ice. With increasing temperature, water molecules gain enough energy to slide over one another in a loose arrangement—a liquid phase. If there is sufficient energy, water molecules escape all association with each other, and they exist as free vapor in the air.

The atmosphere can hold only a limited amount of water vapor. When an air mass has taken on the maximum level that it can hold, the *saturation value* has been reached. The main factor that determines saturation value is temperature: warm air can hold more water than cold air. *Humidity* is the term used to describe the amount of water vapor in the atmosphere. This is usually reported as *relative humidity,* which is defined as the amount of water vapor present in the air compared to its maximum capacity or saturation value. Thus a reading of 75 percent relative humidity means the air contains three quarters of the maximum amount of water vapor it could contain.

When conditions exist that exceed the saturation value, the air becomes overloaded with moisture and water begins to reenter a liquid phase. There are several different ways in

which this phenomenon unfolds. One example, which we will consider now, is the formation of dew.

As the sun warms the earth during the day, large amounts of water vapor enter the atmosphere—especially from the oceans. Water molecules can remain in a gaseous state as long as their energy level is high. When night falls and the air begins to cool, air molecules lose energy, their motion decreases, and they pack closer together. As the temperature continues to fall, the air's capacity to hold water is exhausted, saturation occurs, and the relative humidity reaches 100 percent. The temperature at which this saturation occurs is called the *dew point.*

As the air temperature drops below the dew point, a process called *condensation* takes place. Land surfaces and objects on them cool off rapidly after the sun sets, and their temperature drops below the dew point more rapidly than the surrounding air. The air in contact with these cooler surfaces loses energy, and water molecules group together in a liquid state to condense as tiny droplets. Dew can form on any cool, nonporous surface that is below the current dew point.

Sometimes the dew point is below the freezing temperature of water. In this case, water will condense not as water droplets but as ice crystals to form frost. While dew is actually beneficial to plants, frost can seriously damage many types of crops by freezing their exposed leaves. Farmers try to combat frost with outdoor heaters and with fans that stir up the cold air nearest the ground and blend it with warmer air above. More recently, scientists have engineered a special type of bacterium that interferes with ice crystal formation. This genetically altered microbe is being tested to determine if it can help plants survive during frosty nights.

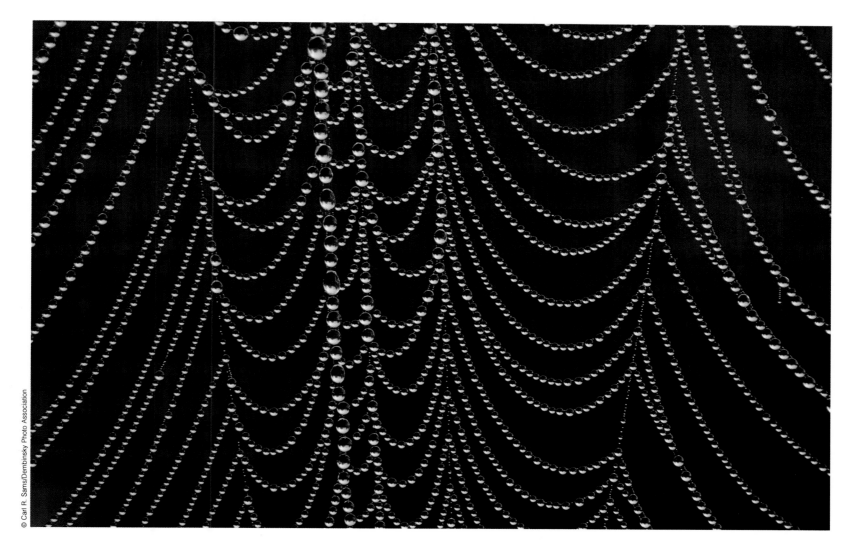

WHY ARE THERE DIFFERENT KINDS OF CLOUDS?

© Stan Osolinski/Dembinsky Photo Association

Clouds are the visible manifestation of water vapor in the atmosphere. Let's first examine the basic mechanism of cloud formation, and then we can appreciate why different types of clouds appear in the sky.

We have already learned that the air around us contains gaseous water that can revert to a liquid state under certain conditions. Water vapor near the ground can condense on cool surfaces to form dew, but most of the water molecules are well above the earth's surface. Even in the air, however, there are tiny particles of dust, smoke, and other debris that can provide a physical base for the formation of tiny water droplets. Such particles are called *condensation nuclei* and are almost always present in the atmosphere.

The most common cause of cloud formation is the rising of warm air that contains moisture. As the sun warms various land regions, the air above is also heated. These warmer air masses are pushed upward into the atmosphere where they begin to expand because of the decrease in pressure. When air expands, its gaseous components move further apart, which reduces the number of collisions between individual molecules. This diminishes their motion, which causes a reduction in their energy level. The net result is that the temperature of the air mass decreases.

There is another factor that often contributes to the cooling of rising air. The warm air masses moving up into the atmosphere usually encounter cooler layers of air that can absorb heat from the rising air and lower their temperature even further.

Both of these cooling phenomena rapidly decrease the overall temperature of the rising air mass. When the temperature falls below the dew point, water molecules begin to condense onto dust particles. These initial seed droplets gradually coalesce into larger and larger conglomerates until finally the air mass is filled with millions of drops of water. Together all this liquid mist becomes thick enough to reflect sunlight and presents to our view the fluffy white image we recognize as a cloud.

Clouds can be categorized into three basic types. *Cirrus* clouds are thin, wispy trails of moisture that occur at high altitudes—about 25,000 feet (7,500 m) and above. The air at this height is very cold, and the dew point is well below freezing, so that water vapor condenses directly into ice crystals. The elongated, streaming appearance of cirrus clouds is caused by the high winds in the upper levels of the atmosphere that blow the ice crystals out into thin streams. The exhaust trails from jet airplanes flying at high altitude can initiate the formation of cirrus clouds. Such exhaust contains water vapor and chemicals that can provide nuclei for condensation. Ice crystals from cirrus clouds can in turn fall into lower regions of the atmosphere to serve as the initial seed for the formation of other cloud types.

Cumulus is the name of the billowing, cauliflower-shaped cloud that grows upward in the sky. These are positioned between 7,000 and 25,000 feet (2,100 and 7,500 m) high. They form when *thermals*—pockets of warm, rising air—push up into the sky and condense out into clouds. Cumulus formations begin with a flat base that marks the level at which the dew point occurs. As thermals rise above this base and cool off, they fold out into puffy billows that build the cloud upward. If the cloud grows high enough, the top will eventually expand out into an anvil shape, indicating it has reached a layer of warmer air near the bottom of the stratosphere. Cumulus clouds that grow to this size are designated *cumulonimbus* and usually bring severe weather conditions—a topic we will turn our attention to in the next section.

The third cloud type is *stratus*, the low-lying sheets of gray that can cover very large regions—occasionally entire continents. They are found in altitudes from approximately 1,000 feet (300 m) above the ground to about 7,000 feet (2,100 m) up.

Examples of cloud formations (clockwise from top left): cumulus, cirrus, cumulonimbus, stratocumulus.

Stratus clouds can form by the even rising of an entire layer of warming air, which is a mild and slow process compared to cumulus formation. This type of cloud can also result from the cooling of lower levels of air by their proximity to an underlying cold land mass. Thus, stratus clouds are common over polar regions where sun-warmed air condenses over the frozen ground.

Condensation of water vapor in the air can also occur at ground level to produce fog. This usually occurs when warm, moisture-laden air comes in contact with cooler areas on the ground. This drops the air temperature below the dew point and water droplets collect into a thick mist. Fog occurs frequently in coastal regions because warm air from inland moves over the cold water where it condenses. Valleys experience more fog than higher areas because the heavy, cooling air tends to sift downward and settle in low-lying pockets. Winds prevent the formation of fog by mixing cold and warm air masses together.

Areas of high pollution tend to have very dense fog because increased debris in the air is available for water to condense on. The infamous London fog grew so thick in December of 1952 that it was impossible to see more than about three feet (1 meter) in any direction. Citizens unknowingly worsened the situation by heating their homes more than was necessary, assuming the heat would "dry out" the wet air, but the burning coal only spewed more dust and chemicals into the air, making the fog even thicker. An estimated 4,000 deaths—from traffic accidents and even people walking into rivers and canals—were attributed to this one episode of fog in London alone. This incident prompted a Clean Air Act that was enacted in 1955 and has since lessened the magnitude of London's fog problems.

© Bart Barlow/Envision

© Christopher C. Bain

WHAT CAUSES LIGHTNING?

MOST CUMULUS FORMATIONS BILLOW UP in the sky during the day and then dissipate quietly at dusk when the cooling earth no longer sends warm thermals up to feed these clouds. Occasionally, large enough amounts of heated, moist air rise up and expand before the cloud system dissipates. This allows a cumulus cloud to achieve *cumulonimbus* stage, at which point it can produce a full-scale thunderstorm.

Conditions within a blossoming cumulonimbus system can become violent and pose a hazard to people both on the ground and in the air. Thermal updrafts grow increasingly stronger, carrying moist air to a high altitude where it condenses into rain or ice crystals. This rapidly cooled, heavy air then falls back toward the earth, creating powerful downdrafts. Strong downward winds are a major concern to airline pilots trying to land—these downward airflows can literally shove the aircraft into the ground as it approaches the runway. When such conditions exist, planes are usually rerouted to another field or held in circling patterns above the airport until weather conditions improve.

Within clouds, water sometimes condenses directly as liquid droplets and then gathers into larger drops to fall as rain. More commonly, moisture condenses in the form of ice crystals in storm clouds. Often this precipitation melts as it falls to earth and turns to rain before reaching the ground. In very severe conditions, falling water droplets are swept back up through the cloud to high altitudes where they freeze and then fall again. As they fall, a layer of moisture condenses on their outer surface, and these droplets can then be swept back up to be refrozen. This cycle can repeat many times before these iceballs, called hailstones, are too heavy to be carried upward by winds and fall to the earth.

Hailstones can be very dangerous and destructive. The largest hailstone on record fell in Coffeyville, Kansas, in 1970. It weighed one and two-thirds pounds (.75 kg) and measured 6.2 inches (15.5 cm) across its diameter—about the size of a cantaloupe. It's not difficult to imagine the damage a rock of ice this large could inflict, but fortunately, most hailstones are much smaller. Still, if you must be outdoors when a hailstorm is forecast, you may want to take along more than just your umbrella: Hailstorms send thousands and thousands of pellets crashing down from the sky at a speed of about 60 miles (37 km) per hour.

In addition to heavy winds and various forms of precipitation, thunderstorms also produce the intriguing electrical event called lightning. The exact mechanism that produces flashes of lightning is not certain: Full-blown storm clouds are not an easy place to carry on scientific experiments. There is, however, a working theory to explain this phenomenon.

The turbulent environment within a storm cloud leads to a separation of charges. Positively charged ions gather in the upper regions of the cloud, while negative particles collect near the bottom (Figure 26). What is responsible for this non-random distribution of charge is not clear, but it is thought to be associated with high winds carrying lighter positively charged material upward, while heavier negative particles fall to the lower regions, carried there by falling water vapor. As this charge separation develops, the cloud is *polarized:* The upper and lower sections exhibit net differences in charge.

The buildup of one type of charged particle in a specific area is an unusual situation. This is because particles of like charge tend to repel each other, while particles of opposite charge tend to attract one another. This causes the polarized cloud to develop a large *electrical potential,* which can be thought of as the force of attraction between positive and negative regions. Finally, this attraction becomes stronger than the forces separating the charged particles, and the potential is discharged in a bolt of lightning.

Lightning begins with a *lead stroke*—a burst of electrons (negatively charged) flowing toward protons (positively charged). About 75 percent of the time these tracks are between charged areas within the cloud. But about 25 percent of lightning races toward the ground, which usually has a net positive charge (Figure 26). This initial stream travels at speeds between 100 and 1,000 miles (160 and 1,600 km) per second. Following this lead stroke, a *return stroke* is directed back along the same path at much greater speed: up to 87,000 miles (139,200 km) per second. This burst of electrical discharge relieves the charge differences, but only temporarily. Conditions within the cloud then regenerate the polarity leading to repeated flashes of lightning.

The flash we see when lightning occurs is the result of atmospheric molecules being *ionized*—broken apart—by the strong electrical current passing through the air. When these molecules are split apart, light is emitted that produces the white streaks that etch across the sky.

The current in a stroke of lightning can reach 200,000 amps —an incredibly strong jolt of electricity. This is enough to raise the temperature of surrounding air to 54,032°F (30,000°C), which is about six times as hot as the surface of the sun. This superheated air expands outward with explosive force, creating shock waves that we hear as thunder. Since the speed of light is so much faster than the speed of sound, we see lightning almost the instant it occurs, while the audible report follows later as a loud clap of thunder.

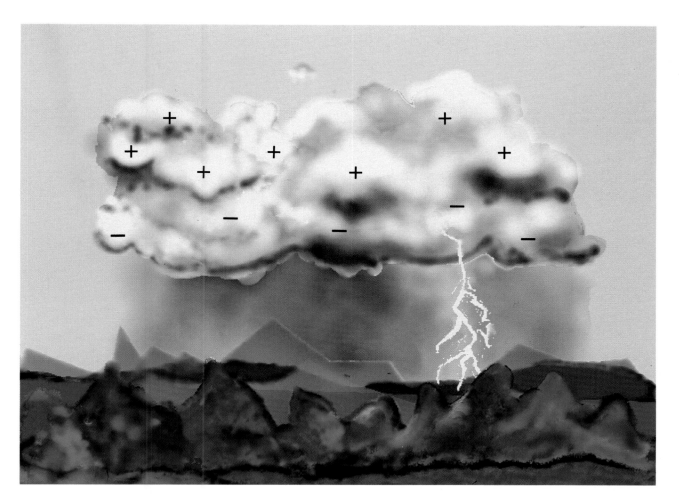

**Figure 26
CONDITIONS THAT PRODUCE LIGHT- NING: Strong winds and other forces within a storm cloud separate positive and negative charges to separate sections. This builds a powerful force that is finally released in an electrical discharge, producing lightning.**

WHAT CAUSES TORNADOES?

THE MOST VIOLENT AND POWERFUL atmospheric disturbances of all are tornadoes. These funnel-shaped windstorms occur mostly along a corridor running through the midwestern United States and arise predominantly during the spring. During an average year, about 600 tornadoes are spotted in this region, which has been nicknamed "Tornado Alley" by meteorologists. The factors that influence the birth of a tornado have been discussed separately in previous sections. Now we will consider how these various forces act in concert to produce this dramatic natural phenomenon.

Global airflow patterns send cold dry air down from polar regions to sweep southward across the central United States on a fairly regular basis. During the spring as the sun aligns more directly over the equator and heats the central belt with increasing efficiency, warm moist air pushes farther and farther northward into the central U.S. In the month of April, these

two air masses push with greatest force toward each other, meeting on the open plains territory of this region (Figure 27).

The interface between these colliding air masses is a volatile zone of extremes in air pressure that produces strong thunderstorm activity. A low pressure area forms when warm moist air rises swiftly, expands, and then contacts cold air overhead. This cooled moist air, along with condensed moisture, then drops rapidly back toward the ground. This pattern creates strong updrafts in the center of the low pressure area and powerful downdrafts toward the outside perimeter. As the storm develops, individual streams of upward flowing air tend to group together, as do downdrafts, strengthening this cycle of airflow until very strong vertical winds are produced. As winds intensify, more and more air is drawn up through the center of the system, which further lowers pressure in the central column, so that the process begins to feed upon itself.

At this point the storm system is very large, covering many square miles (or square kilometers) and exhibiting severe winds. But a tornado does not form, even under these extreme conditions, until the winds begin to spin. What initiates this spin to create a vortex is not fully understood, but a clue comes from the observation that almost all tornadoes rotate in a counterclockwise direction. Recall that the Coriolis effect is responsible for global wind patterns. The major winds blowing across the central U.S. are the westerlies, which bend in a counterclockwise motion. These winds are thought to be responsible for twisting updrafts into circling patterns.

Once started, the twirling column begins rotating faster and faster. This is caused by a drop of pressure inside the tube which generates an inward pull that is countered by an outer force due to rotation. This results in the sides of the column effectively excluding air from entering the central shaft: The only means of entrance is through the bottom opening. Air is sucked up through this lower opening, amplifying the updraft, which increases the speed of rotation even more.

Eventually, this process reduces the column to a diameter of one-half mile (.8 km) or less, with a concurrent increase of wind speeds that may approach 200 miles (320 km) per hour. In its final stage, the funnel becomes visible because of water vapor that has condensed due to the low pressure inside the column. This funnel is pulled downward by its rotating winds and can contact the ground.

When tornadoes touch down, nothing in their path is safe. The force of high-speed wind obliterates most structures, but it is not the only source of destruction. When the extreme low pressure center passes over buildings and houses, these structures literally blow apart as the higher pressure inside explodes outward.

Figure 27
TORNADO ALLEY
(left): During the spring of each year, cold wind coming down from the arctic and warm, humid air flowing up from the Gulf of Mexico meet in the central plains. This collision spawns numerous tornadoes in the region.

© Brian Parker/Tom Stack & Associates

Tornadoes that touch down cause total destruction, left, leaving nothing but rubble and debris in their trail.

WHY ARE THERE DESERTS?

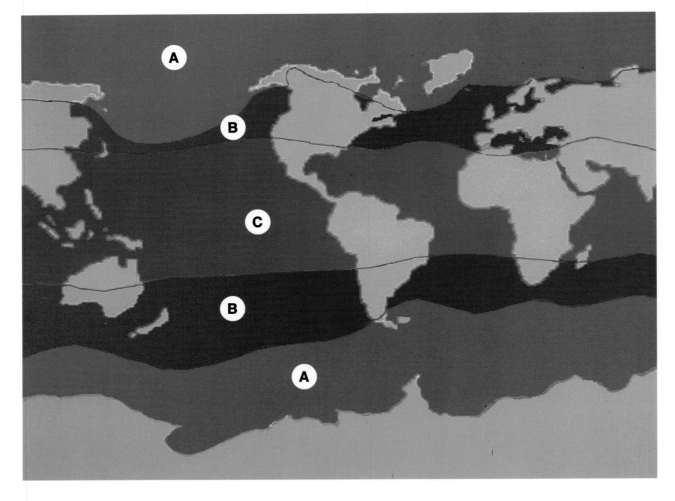

CLIMATE IS DEFINED as the prevailing weather conditions that exist in a region averaged over a period of several years. Although most areas of the world experience seasonal variation during the year, the pattern of these changes is consistent and predictable over time. Let's first identify those factors that influence climate and the general climatic zones that cover the earth. Then we will take a detailed look at the conditions that cause one of the most interesting climate types found on earth: deserts.

The most important determinant of the climate in a particular region is the amount and intensity of solar radiation it receives. Since the equatorial zone is aligned nearly perpendicular to the sun's rays, efficient heating of this region produces the highest average temperatures on the planet. This central belt also has only minor fluctuations in daylight hours during the various seasons, which maintains the average temperature at about 79°F (26°C) throughout the year. At the north and south poles, sunlight reaches the earth at an extremely slanted angle resulting in only modest warming. For large portions of the year, there are only a few hours of daylight. This minimal amount of sunlight keeps the average temperature in these regions well below freezing. Regions between the poles and the equator receive an intermediate level of solar radiation. These areas experience significant

changes in the amount of sunlight received over the year and thus have wide shifts in average daily temperature.

Another important feature that affects climate is altitude. Layers of air high above the earth's surface are warmed less efficiently than air near the ground. Areas of high altitude such as mountainous regions that protrude up into layers of cooler air consistently experience lower daily temperatures than surrounding plains and valleys.

Winds also play a major role in determining climate. The global wind belts push air masses across much of the earth's surface, bringing warm or cool air to affect the temperature of a region. These wind patterns are also the means by which water in the form of vapor and precipitation is transported inland to the major land masses.

The amount of rainfall in a particular region has a major impact on its climate. As mentioned above, the earth's airflow system in various latitudes is the major factor in the global pattern of annual precipitation. In general, the zones of heaviest rain are the equator and latitudes between 40 degrees and 55 degrees in both hemispheres.

The terrain of a region can also be a factor in climatic conditions. Large flat land masses heat the air above them efficiently, which raises the average temperature as well as promoting low pressure systems with subsequent precipitation. Mountains can disrupt wind patterns and cause moist air to rise and condense as winds push up their slopes. This often creates a *rain shadow* on the downwind side of mountain ranges where conditions are dryer and warmer than they are on the other side, which receives moist air.

Ocean currents also influence climate by circulating warm or cool water past land masses. The northwestern part of Europe enjoys a warmer climate than its northern latitude usually allows. This is possible because a warm ocean current, the North Atlantic drift, brings warm water along the coast that in turn heats the offshore air. This warmer air is then pushed inland by the prevailing westerly winds.

All of these factors coordinate to produce the earth's climatic zones, which are shown in Figure 28. The equatorial belt exhibits *tropical* climates that are characterized by steady high temperatures, low winds, and heavy precipitation—more than 100 inches (2.5 m) of rain annually. Outside this central belt are the *middle latitude* climates where medium temperatures and seasonal variations dominate. At the highest latitudes are *polar* climates where extreme cold is the main feature.

Within these major divisions, a wide diversity of specialized climates exists. An example is deserts, which are defined as land regions with low levels of available moisture. Deserts sponsor growth of only the most hearty and rugged types of plants, many of which are specially adapted to survive on only trace amounts of water for long periods.

An interesting combination of factors produces deserts. An examination of Figure 29 reveals that they cluster in regions near 30 degrees latitude in both hemispheres—the Horse Latitudes—where descending dry air masses bring only minor amounts of moisture down. Most deserts are located on the western edge of continents next to cold ocean currents. These cold waters keep the air above them cooled, which lowers the air's capacity to hold water vapor. Thus when this dry ocean air moves inland across deserts, it contains no significant moisture to dump as rain. In addition, many of these arid regions are edged by mountain ranges that strip any moist winds of their precipitation before they pass over the desert area. These factors keep deserts isolated from significant rainfall and produce the characteristic dry features associated with this type of terrain.

We don't think of polar ice caps as deserts but technically they fit the definition. These regions are so cold that all of the water is solidified and thus unavailable for use. This fact along with very low temperatures turns polar regions into frozen wastelands where it is difficult for any life forms to survive.

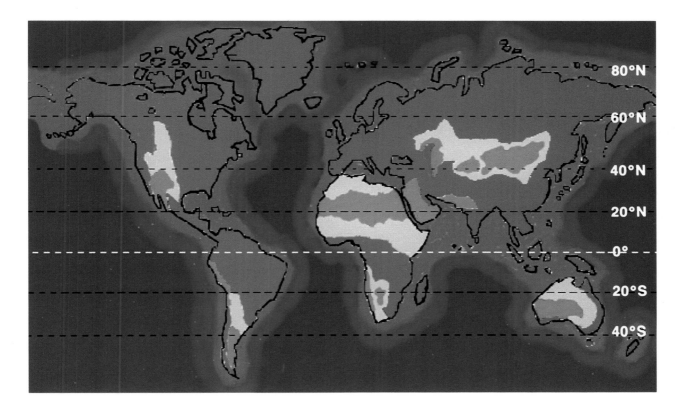

**Figure 29
DESERT REGIONS
OF THE WORLD:**
Most deserts (shown in orange) and semideserts (shown in yellow) are found near 30 degrees latitude north or south and are close to oceans or bordered by large mountain ranges.

WHAT CAUSES DROUGHTS?

BECAUSE SO MANY DIFFERENT FACTORS influence the earth's weather conditions, the climate of some regions is a delicate balance that can be altered by minor changes in one or more of the contributing forces. We occasionally hear of record high or low temperatures for a given location on a specific day. This occurs when typical weather patterns for that region are interrupted by a severe cold front or heat wave or some other event that temporarily overrides the normal set of controlling factors.

One of the most crucial parameters of climate is the amount of precipitation an area receives during the year. The many different life forms of a region are adapted to the amount and timing of rainfall, and long-term reductions in precipitation can adversely effect fragile ecosystems that rely on a regular supply of water. Let's first examine the mechanism of water distribution over the earth, and then we will consider the factors which alter the level of yearly precipitation that result in drought conditions.

An estimated 95,000 cubic miles (390,000 cubic km) of water circulates between the atmosphere and the earth's surface every year. This cycle begins with water evaporating into the air, 85 percent of which comes from the world's oceans. The other 15 percent is contributed by lakes and rivers and from plants and the upper layer of soil on the ground. This huge amount of water is carried by global winds to various points around the planet, where it returns to earth in the form of rain, snow, dew, and other forms of precipitation.

An average of 40 inches (100 cm) of rain falls on the earth's surface from the skies every year, but its distribution is extremely uneven. Some desert regions receive less than an inch of rain during the entire year, while sections of Hawaii are bombarded with close to 500 inches (1,250 cm) of rain annually. Most rainfall—about 75 percent—lands directly back in the oceans. Another 10 percent collects in streams, rivers, and lakes, while the remaining 15 percent soaks into the earth to become ground water. Although water that falls on land remains as surface or ground water for some period of time, it eventually flows back into the sea to complete the water cycle.

A drought occurs when the level of rainfall in a particular region is significantly reduced for a long period of time—usually several years in a row—to the extent that ecological processes are disrupted. Most droughts occur in arid regions, where water supplies are already critically limited and even minor reductions in vital precipitation upset the fragile environment.

One factor that can produce drought conditions is a high-pressure system that stalls and remains in the same location for an extended period of time. Normally, pressure systems travel in regular cycles across land masses. High pressure areas bring with them dry, heavy air accompanied by cloudless skies—not the conditions for a good rainstorm. If a large high-pressure system becomes stationary over a region, particularly during the months of heaviest precipitation, drastic reductions in the year's total rainfall can result.

A shift in wind patterns can also produce droughts. Some regions receive their moisture from air masses blown overhead by specific wind systems. A slight change in the course of these winds can direct moisture around the affected region, leaving it dry. The severe drought that hit the northeastern U.S. from 1962 to 1967 was caused by a change in the typical airflow pattern in this region. Normally, moist warm air from the Gulf of Mexico flows northward over this region, where it runs into southward flowing cold air from Canada. This collision causes the warm air mass to cool off and drop its load of water. But starting in 1962, the cool air mass from Canada did not extend far enough south to contact the warm air, which migrated out over the Atlantic Ocean before emptying its content of moisture.

This pattern continued for five seasons causing serious water shortages in New York and hundreds of other cities. Many lakes and streams completely disappeared. Heavy snow and rain in the winter of 1967 brought substantial relief, but the lesson was learned. Citizens and public officials got serious about water conservation, and programs were initiated to better store available water during times of plenty.

Man's handling of the environment can also contribute to droughts. The Dust Bowl of the 1930s that devastated an area covering 50 million acres (20 million hectares) across the plains and southwestern United States was caused by a combination of reduced rainfall and large-scale cultivation. The natural flora of this region are field grasses that send deep roots into the ground which tend to hold soil in place. Settlers plowed under this vegetation, replacing it with various crops. The loose soil and short-rooted plants could not withstand the onslaught of reduced moisture and high winds that afflicted this area from 1930 to 1937. During the final stages of this disaster, wind storms reduced visibility to near zero and carried dust to locations more than 1,000 miles (1,600 km) away. The topsoil was completely blown away over much of this region, leaving a barren wasteland unfit for growing anything.

Currently, the large-scale stripping of tropical rain forests on the South American continent poses a potential alteration in the earth's climate as a whole. The daily burning of thousands of acres (or hectares) of thick woodlands sends huge amounts of material into the air and may lead to a significant temperature increase over the planet. The impact of this slash-and-burn clearing of the earth's tropical forests on the planet's delicate ecosystems remains to be seen.

The plains and southwest United States experienced a devastating drought, left, during the 1930s. The Dust Bowl was caused by both reduced rainfall and large-scale cultivation. Large portions of rain forests in Central and South America, below, are cleared by complete burning every day.

© FPG International

© Wendy Shattil/Bob Rozinski/Tom Stack & Associates

THE CHANGING EARTH

HOW DO RIVERS CHANGE COURSE?

THE RIVERS OF THE WORLD carry approximately 8,000 cubic miles (33,000 cubic km) of water to the sea every year. Creeks and small streams number in the hundreds of thousands and can be found in all types of terrain, but the bulk of the earth's surface water eventually joins into less than a dozen major rivers. For example, about half of the continental United States is drained by just one river system—the mighty Mississippi.

The world's longest river, the Nile, winds a 4,160 mile (6,656 km) long path northward through the African continent to reach the Mediterranean Sea. In total volume, the largest waterway on the planet is the Amazon. It begins in the Andes Mountains in Peru on the western edge of South America and flows east across the entire continent to empty into the Atlantic Ocean. In this equatorial region, the Amazon drains the huge rain forests, which receive hundreds of inches (or centimeters) of precipitation annually. All of this rainfall feeds into the Amazon and swells its borders to an incredible width: By the time it reaches the ocean, this river measures 200 miles (320 km) across. About one-fifth of the world's total volume of fresh surface water flows through the Amazon and pushes so far out into the Atlantic that nearly 200 miles (320 km) out in the ocean past the river's mouth, the water is still fresh, not salty.

Most rivers get their start in high mountainous regions where water runs swiftly downhill under the force of gravity.

One source of these initial small streams is the snow or ice packs on mountain peaks that melt during warm seasons, sending water trickling down the slopes. Other rivers begin from lakes that overflow or have a constant outlet. Glaciers are another source of water that develops into rivers. Water that soaks into mountains and then runs underground can also be a source of streams when it leaks out onto hard, nonporous material and flows above ground.

As tiny streams journey downhill, they are always directed to the lowest point by the force of gravity. Since the ground is rarely smooth, a stream's path is usually crooked, bending and weaving with the contour of the land. This pattern directs many separate streams into a common low-lying channel where they join to form larger arteries. A stream that connects into a larger water system is called a *tributary*, and it is the constant influx of water from many separate tributaries that builds a tiny mountain stream into a large river. The Amazon has approximately 1,100 individual tributaries, some of them over 1,000 miles (1,600 km) long.

The force of so much water moving across the earth's surfaces causes *erosion*, a process that wears down the land and ultimately carries it out to sea. Water dissolves many different kinds of soil and rock efficiently, breaking them down to be swept along by the moving current. In this way, the world's highlands are constantly being eroded and transferred to lower

The Mississippi River Delta, right, is criss-crossed by many streams that change course often as silt builds up.

Aerial view of the Green River, right, in Canyonlands National Park, southeast Utah.

© Manfred Gottschalk/Tom Stack & Associates

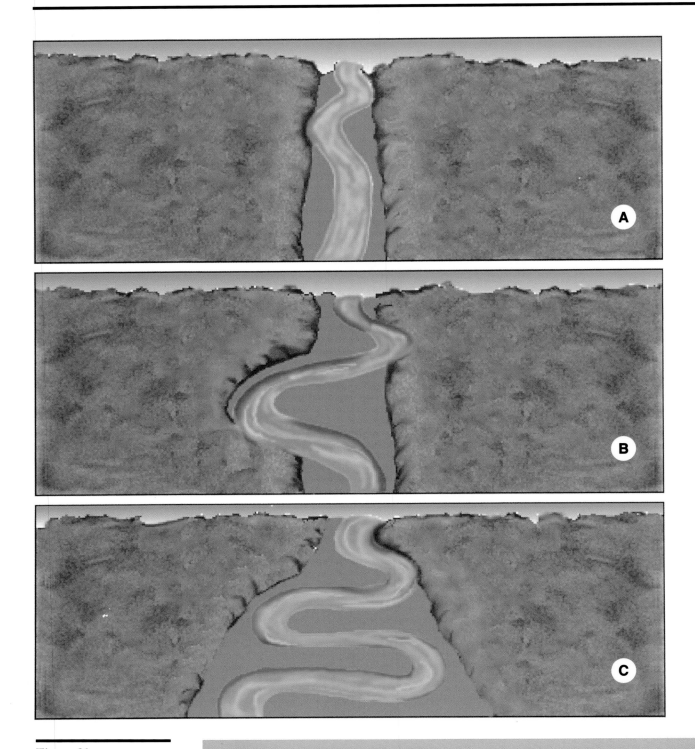

Figure 30
DEVELOPMENT OF
CURVES IN A RIVER
(left): Erosion at the outer edge of slight bends
in a river's course
eventually increases
the curve and moves
the path of water flow.

Figure 31
ISOLATION OF A
RIVER LOOP (right):
Erosion at the edges
of a looping section
can eventually break
through and meet. This
action sends most of the
water past the loop, which
is eventually sealed off
from the river to form
an independent lake.

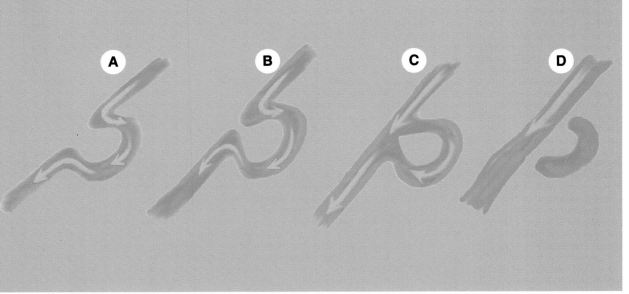

regions. Were it not for geologic remodeling forces such as volcanoes and earthquakes that push up new mountain ranges, erosion would completely flatten the planet's land masses in about 20 million years.

On a smaller scale, rivers are responsible for sculpturing the earth by carving out deep valleys and canyons. The Colorado River has produced the deepest valley in the world, the Grand Canyon, which is over one mile (1.6 km) deep in some places. Very large rivers can also reshape the earth's surface by building new territories called deltas. These are mounds of built up sand and gravel that are deposited at the mouths of rivers where the river water meets the ocean water and slows down.

The degree of erosion for specific areas depends on several factors and is not simply a matter of the size of rivers in the area. The highest amount of erosion on earth occurs in Southeast Asia, where material from the rapidly decaying Himalayas is transported to the ocean. The major rivers in this area, the Ganges, Irrawaddy, Mekong, Jangzi, and Huang all deposit several thousand tons of material into the ocean every year.

Many rivers change course from time to time. The mechanism by which this occurs is illustrated in Figure 30. Any curve or bend is prone to exaggeration by the force of water flowing through that point. Since the water flowing along the outside of the curve has a longer distance to travel than water moving on the inside of the curve, the outer edge experiences a faster current and thus heavier erosion. Water at the inner border of the curve tends to slow down and drop silt and other sediments, building up the shore on this inside edge. This process amplifies the bend, moving it outward from the main course and producing a *meandering* river that winds back and forth rather than running in a straight line. This pattern is typical of slow-moving rivers that cross relatively flat terrain.

If two adjacent curves or *meanders* progress toward each other, they can eventually break through the dividing land barrier and join, as illustrated in Figure 31. This produces an island surrounded by a loop of slow-moving water. Eventually this looping structure can be separated into an isolated body of water called an *oxbow lake* or *horseshoe lake*. This occurs because the current slows as it enters the loop, dumping sand that builds up and finally divides the river from the newly formed lake.

Rivers can also change course by breaking through a barrier between two closely aligned waterways or by shifting into a lower-lying valley nearby. In addition, earthquakes can disrupt the course of rivers by raising or lowering land masses to detour the flow of water through a certain region. Volcanoes, too, substantially alter normal avenues of water flow by laying down new rock layers that impede and sidetrack preexisting rivers.

Deltas are characterized by frequent course changes. Large amounts of silt pile up in the river's path as it slows at ocean level. This can quickly block the main channel and divert the major flow off in another direction almost overnight.

Aerial view of the Russel Fork River in Virginia.

WHAT IS QUICKSAND?

QUICKSAND IS AN INTERESTING PHENOMENON that most of us have learned about only through movies and television. As Hollywood would have it, there is not a more deceptive pitfall for hero and villain alike than a patch of oozing moist sand that can swallow its victim in a matter of seconds. Such portrayals tend to be overdramatized, but it is indeed possible for animals and people to sink into pools of wet mud and sand. Knowing the basic features of quicksand, however, and how to behave if accidently caught in it, can prevent serious harm.

The main places that quicksand is found are along the banks of rivers and lakes where deposits of sand and gravel are soaked from below by a constant influx of water from a spring (Figure 32). It can also form out in the middle of rivers where the topography and current lay down sand bars and ribbons of silt just under the water's surface. Even a river bed that is for the most part dry can harbor patches of sand that are moistened from underneath by springs. Under these conditions, pockets of loose, wet sand can form which have a consistency that will not support heavy objects.

It is thought that the texture and shape of the sand in these areas is an important factor in the formation of quicksand. Fine sand particles have a slick surface and rounded shape from the polishing action that occurs when they tumble over miles (or kilometers) of rocky river bottoms. These smooth grains of sand get slippery when wet, lowering their capacity to support weight.

When you step into quicksand, the sand particles tend to slide over one another and give way so that you sink. This sinking action is augmented by motion, so that the harder you struggle and thrash about, the faster and farther you sink. The important thing to remember then, is that if you do wander into quicksand, the worst thing to do is start fighting to get out. There is only one way to sink in completely over your head, and that is to panic.

If you just hold still, you will only sink in part way and then stop. This is because the density of quicksand is higher than the density of your body. Just as you can float in a swimming pool because the water has a higher density than your body, so water laden with sand is more dense than you are. At some point, an equilibrium will occur where enough of your weight is suspended in the surrounding wet sand that the collective material beneath will be able to support you.

Getting out of quicksand can be difficult because its sticky, viscous texture counters every attempt to pull up out of it. In addition, there is no support below to thrust against. Tree limbs or other objects that have a large surface area will not sink very fast; these can be laid over the sand and used for leverage to climb out. Alternatively, rope can be used to pull out someone stuck in quicksand, or a companion with a firm position on solid ground can serve as a foundation to pull against. This means it is a good idea not to wander around by yourself in areas where quicksand might be. But the best strategy of all is to watch where you're stepping.

Figure 32
FORMATION OF QUICKSAND: A) Conditions for generation of quicksand include buildup of sand at the edge of a body of water, fed from below by natural springs; **B)** in some cases, a sandbar is formed that extends above the surface when the water level drops; **C)** a dry crust can form over quicksand, making it appear solid.

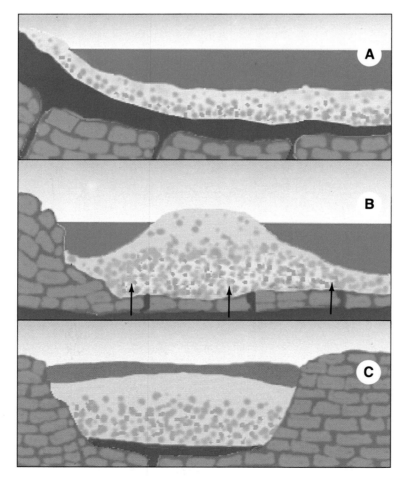

© Martin Harvey/The Wildlife Collection

© Boyd Norton

Pockets of quicksand can be found in the Namib Desert of Namibia in southern Africa, above, as well as in Utah in the western United States, left.

HOW DOES A NATURAL SPRING FORM?

A FULL TWO THIRDS of the precipitation that falls on the earth's land masses soaks into the ground. This process is enhanced by vegetation—especially grasses and other ground cover—that hold water in place while it has a chance to sink into the earth. The angle of the ground is also a factor. Steep slopes drain so quickly that most rainfall doesn't have time to pass under the surface, while flatter lands have a much longer time period to soak up moisture. The temperature and humidity also influence the effectiveness of absorption: If low humidity and warm temperatures follow closely after a rainstorm, much of the moisture deposited on the ground will evaporate back into the atmosphere before it has a chance to move down into the soil.

The nature and composition of the *strata* or layers of dirt and rock below the earth's surface control the rate at which water moves deeper into the ground. Certain types of soil that are sandy or made up of other small particulate matter exhibit a high degree of *porosity*, which means water can pass through it quite easily. Harder substances such as slate, granite, and metamorphic rock are nearly impenetrable and strongly impede the downward seepage of water. But even in very hard rock layers, there are usually cracks and gaps that allow some water to pass.

Water will continue to be pulled downward into the earth by the force of gravity until it reaches a rock stratum it cannot permeate. Here it will collect and spread into the surrounding area to form a *zone of saturation* (Figure 33). The top border of this saturation zone forms the *water table*, which is how deep a well must be sunk in order to obtain fresh water. The distance below the ground of the water table varies widely from one area to another. In some low-lying valleys, it is literally just a few inches (or centimeters) beneath the surface, while in certain mountainous terrains that receive little precipitation it can be over one thousand feet (300 m) below ground. In addition, the water table of a particular area can fluctuate over time in response to the amount of rainfall.

When the contour of the land dips below the level of the water table, groundwater leaks out of the ground to form a natural spring as shown in Figure 33. Thus mountain slopes are the most common location of springs, where the water table intersects the ground surface. Springs usually feed into streams, rivers, or lakes, although some flow only a short distance before sinking back into the ground at a point where the water table is lower.

Some springs exit out of the side of cliffs to form small waterfalls. In regions where winters are severe, the ground water can get cold enough to freeze. Here, the spring water flowing out of steep rock walls crystallizes into shimmering trails of ice, as if still cascading in frozen splendor down the rocky face of the cliffs.

Most groundwater is maintained at a fairly constant temperature—very near the average temperature of the atmosphere in the corresponding region. In some locations, groundwater travels deep into the earth where it is heated by molten rock called *magma*. This warmer groundwater dissolves surrounding substances more efficiently than cold water and thus contains elevated levels of various minerals—especially calcium carbonate, a major component of limestone and marble. When heated water makes its way to the surface, it forms a *thermal spring*, also called a *hot spring*. When the hot water of these springs reaches the surface and cools off, some of the dissolved calcium carbonate or *calcite* is deposited at the mouth of the spring to form layers that build up over time. Fresh deposits are whitish at first but tend to discolor with time as various contaminants such as iron and sulphur compounds are laid down.

These unusual springs are often turned into resorts where people come to bathe in the highly mineralized environment. Some visitors are convinced that these rare waters have medicinal properties and that soaking in them can stimulate the body's healing functions. Certain minerals dissolved in spring water such as sodium and magnesium sulfate do in fact display certain physiological activities, but it is difficult to assess the effect of floating around in dilute mixtures of these compounds. Perhaps the main benefit comes from the soothing and relaxing feeling provided by immersing one's self in a pool of warm water.

Natural spring water from a number of places around the world is bottled and sold as exceptional drinking water. Some springs contain significant natural carbonation that manufacturers use as a base to formulate beverages. In Japan and Iceland, hot springs are exploited as a source of heat for warming homes and other buildings. Some of the very hottest springs, with water temperatures near boiling, have been harnessed for the production of *geothermal power*. In this process, steam is captured and used to generate electricity. Thus, natural springs are not only an interesting natural phenomenon but are also used directly in several beneficial ways.

Figure 33
NATURAL STRATA:
A) Top soil; B) porous rock; C) water table; D) zone of saturation; E) non-porous rock; and F) segment of non-porous rock that directs water to the surface to form a spring.

A hot spring in Kootenay National Park, British Columbia.

WHAT IS A GEYSER?

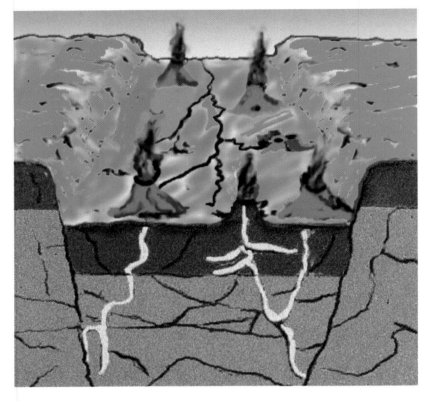

HYDROTHERMAL ACTIVITY—THE PROCESS that exudes hot water and steam from the earth—occurs in many locations around the world and in several different geologic settings. Most hot springs and thermal vents are found in regions associated with recent volcanic activity, though a few exceptions are known: The Hot Springs in Arkansas and White Sulfur Springs in Virginia lie in areas where volcanoes have not been active for millions of years. In these cases, groundwater may settle very deep into the earth where it is heated and then returned up to the surface by a syphoning action where the spring forms.

Thermal vents also protrude from the ocean floor, spewing extremely hot water out into the surrounding cold sea. This creates a fascinating and unique environment—a small pocket of warm, mineral-rich water deep in the ocean surrounded by near freezing water. Such regions are the habitat of intriguing life forms that are specifically adapted to this precarious environment. Biologists have recently isolated new organisms from these vent regions which have special biochemical properties that allow them to survive in the extreme heat conditions present at these sites.

Geysers are a special type of hot spring that periodically expels steam and boiling water. They usually occur in sunken flat regions that are called *geyser basins* (Figure 34). The strata underlying such basins are made up of hardened, nonporous compounds. These rock layers develop cracks and gaps that form channels coursing up through the rock formations.

The structural features that produce a geyser are a restricted main tube running up to the surface and connecting expanded pockets feeding into it (Figure 34). The geyser's cycle begins with groundwater migrating into the deep fissures linked to the main channel. This water collects in ballooned areas where it is in contact with surrounding heated rock and thus gets hotter and hotter.

Under standard conditions, water begins vaporizing at a temperature of 212°F (100°C). But at the bottom of a column 200 feet (60 m) high, water does not boil until it reaches a temperature of 329°F (165°C). This is because the increased pressure forces the water molecules to remain close together, even though they are moving rapidly from absorbed heat energy.

The water deep underground in a geyser tube is under high pressure from the weight of all the water above it—typically 500 feet (150 m) or more. In addition, the connections between adjoining passages are often narrow, so that water cannot circulate extensively. This means heat transfer is restricted, so that deep water cannot mix with cooler water above to release heat energy. All this leads to superheating of water deep within the geyser and a tremendous buildup of trapped energy.

Eventually the superheated and pressurized water reaches the boiling point. As a liquid evaporates into a gas, it expands rapidly. When the water deep in a geyser finally vaporizes, it bursts into steam with explosive power. This forces the contents of the internal cavities in the only direction possible—out into the main channel and up through the geyser tube, pushing water ahead of it. The result is a blast of steam and water that spouts out of the geyser's mouth and high into the air. This eruption releases the built up pressure within the geyser, which then calms down until another buildup repeats the episode.

One of the best geyser basins in the world is located in Yellowstone Park in Wyoming. About 200 separate spouts can be found in this area, including perhaps the most famous of all: Old Faithful. This structure was named because of the clockwork schedule of its eruptions, blasting water 120 feet (36 m) into the air every sixty-five minutes. Most geysers' cycles are more sporadic and can vary in occurrence from every few minutes to only once in several weeks.

Some geysers last for only a short time. In 1901, the biggest geyser on record appeared in New Zealand, but lasted for only two years. Eruptions measured up to 1,500 feet (450 m) high and spewed out not just water but mud and occasionally large rocks. It eventually ceased erupting, presumably because its tubes and channels deteriorated, leaving ordinary crumbled strata saturated with groundwater.

Figure 34
GEYSER BASIN (left):
Geysers are usually
found in a sunken
region where cracks in
underlying rock form
channels to the surface.

Castle Geyser, right,
is one of about 200
geysers found in Yellow-
stone National Park.

© Michael Francis/The Wildlife Collection

HOW ARE CAVES FORMED?

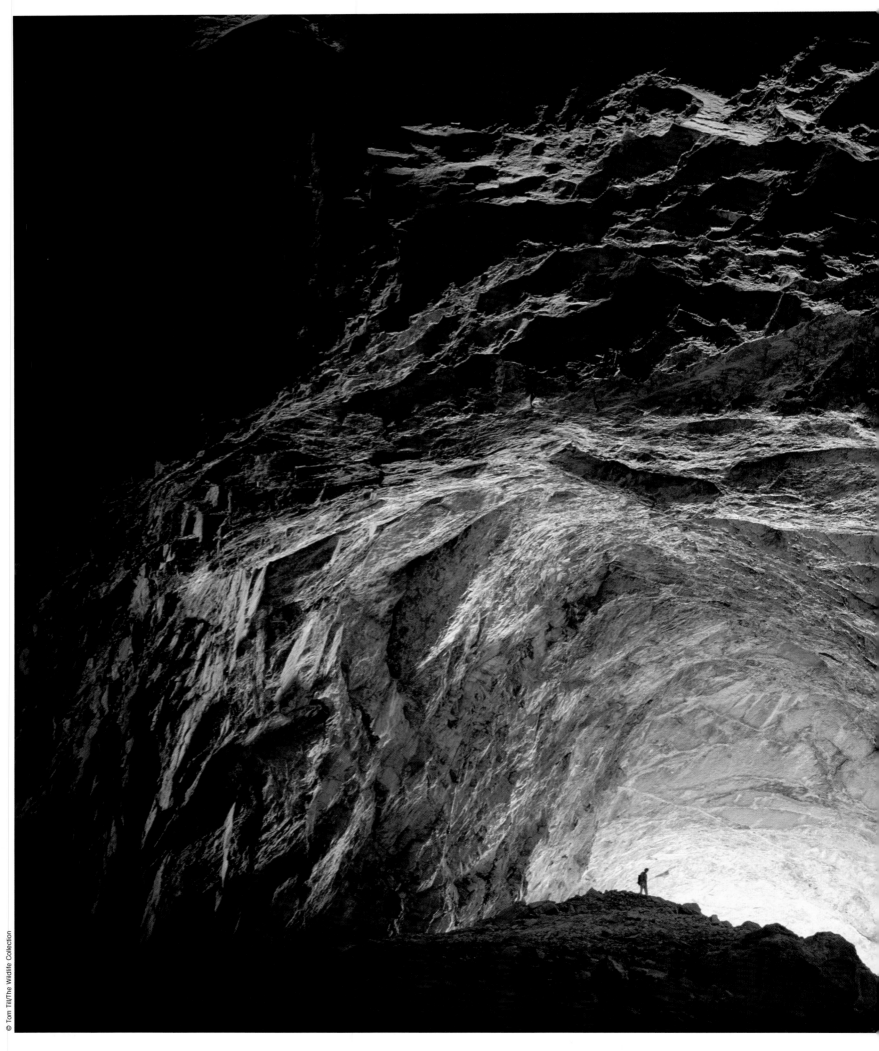

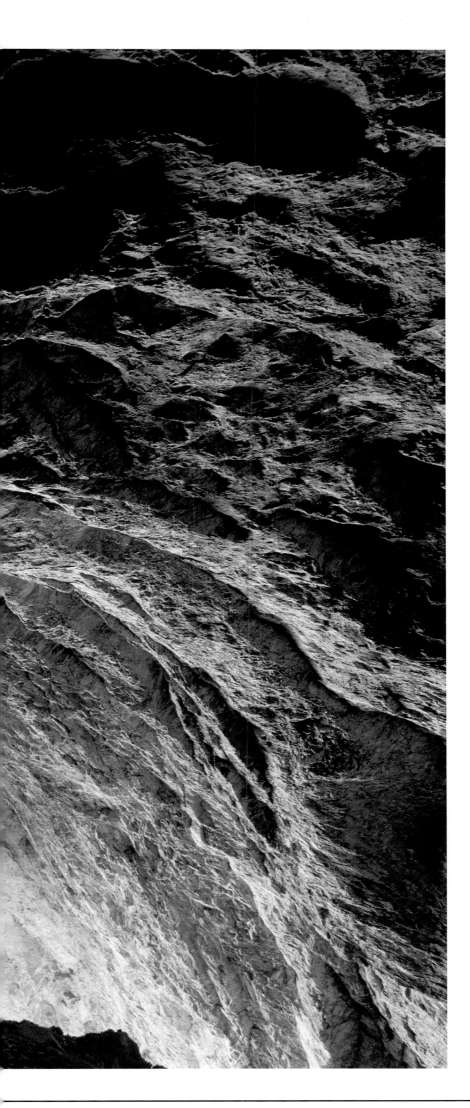

HAVE YOU HEARD THE PHRASE "standing on solid ground" used to convey assurance or stability? Ironically, in some regions of the world, the ground beneath us is not very solid at all—its texture is more like Swiss cheese, with channels and holes coursing in all directions. These eerie and mysterious caves are the product of erosion operating below the surface of the land masses of the world. In this section, we will consider the forces that excavate the "solid ground" deep within the earth and hollow it out into spectacular caverns that are truly phenomenal to experience.

Every year about 3,600 cubic miles (15,000 cubic km) of water sinks into the ground and then slowly migrates through the earth toward the ocean. This huge amount of groundwater does not pass without effect. Just as streams and rivers transport tons of material to the sea, water flowing underground also carves out passages and carries material away.

Water alone can dissolve many substances found in various rock formations. But this property is enhanced by *carbon dioxide* (CO_2), a gas picked up from the atmosphere as rain falls through the sky before soaking into the ground. CO_2 dissolves in water to form *carbonic acid*, a compound that amplifies the eroding capability of water about twenty-five fold when it contacts certain materials.

The type of rock that is particularly susceptible to erosion by groundwater is *limestone*. This is a soft, fine-grained sedimentary rock consisting mainly of *calcite*, a compound that dissolves relatively well in water containing carbonic acid. A close examination of limestone reveals it is made up of the shells of tiny sea animals. Calcite, which is present in high levels in these shells, gives them strength and hardness. Beds of limestone are created on the bottom surface of oceans when the remains of billions of tiny creatures pile up over long periods of time to form layers that eventually petrify into rock. These deposits are then lifted up by geologic reshaping forces such as earthquakes to become part of land masses. Limestone is abundant in the earth's crust and is found in many parts of the world.

Under the ground's surface, limestone deposits in contact with water erode away to produce channels and tunnels as illustrated in Figure 35. This is a slow process that can take thousands or even millions of years. Over such long periods, the path of underground water flow can also change, which empties out the cavity, classifying it as a cave.

Leviathan cave in the Worthington Mountains of Nevada is made of limestone.

Figure 35
FORMATION OF A CAVE: (A) As a river erodes deeper and deeper into the earth, water begins seeping sideways into porous rock. (B) Erosion eventually dissolves softer materials, which are carried away by the river. (C) When the water level drops below this dissolved porous level, water drains out of the hollowed area, producing a cave.

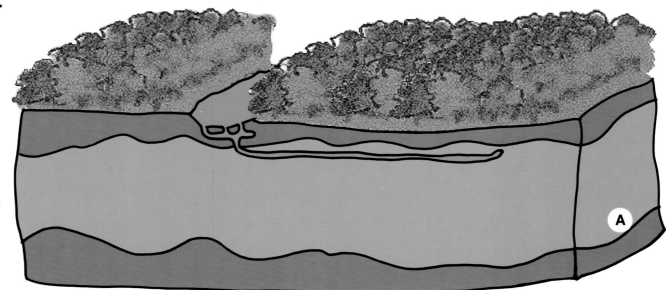

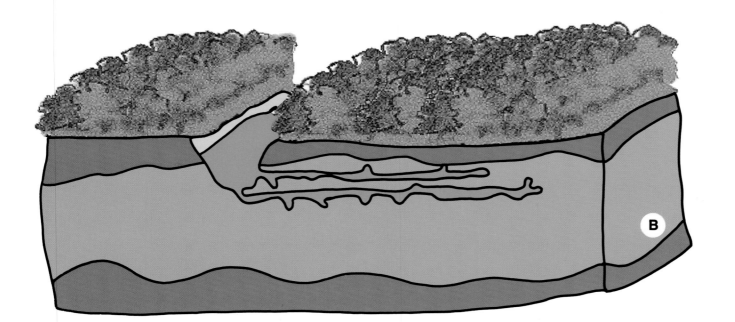

Due to the process which forms them, caves are usually very damp places and often have streams trickling along the floor and water dripping from the ceiling. The mineral-laden drips from the top of caves tend to form *stalactites,* which are projections of deposited calcium carbonate hanging down from the roof like icicles (Figure 36). They form and grow because some of the calcite dissolved in water leaking through the limestone ceiling precipitates out onto the surrounding rock. As more and more calcite is deposited, an extended finger-shaped structure forms, growing downward toward the floor. The water that drips off this structure strikes the floor of the cave below and can deposit calcium carbonate there as well. This produces a spike of rock pointing upward called a *stalagmite.* If stalactites and stalagmites continue to grow toward each other, they can fuse to form a continuous column. All these structures add a haunting, unnatural tone to the appearance of underground caverns.

The ceiling of limestone caves can erode to the point that the top soil above is no longer supported and collapses. This creates a *sinkhole,* which marks the end of the cave process.

The dimensions of some of the world's caves are remarkable. The longest known tunnels are the Mammoth Caves in Kentucky, measuring 236 miles (378 km). Caves in Russia, Spain, and France all drop over 4,300 feet (1,290 m) below the ground. The largest known cavern was discovered in 1981 in Borneo. It measures 2,300 feet (690 m) long by 1,300 feet (390 m) wide—large enough to contain seventeen football fields—and the ceiling is over 200 feet (60 m) high.

Although erosion of limestone deposits is responsible for the formation of most caves, there are other ways they can be created. The action of waves along rocky coastlines wears away softer underlying sediments in cliffs to form sea caves. Wind-blown sand can burrow into mountainsides to create shallow indentations. Such caves provided shelter for early Indian tribes in the southwestern U.S. who made their homes in wind caves. Glaciers also exhibit caves. These are formed by uneven melting within the glacier, which forms spectacular icy tunnels that can collapse without warning, making them very dangerous.

Volcanic activity is sometimes responsible for cave formation. The exterior surface of a lava flow can cool off and solidify while molten rock continues to flow through the interior passage. If the internal flow empties out before cooling off, a cave is formed. The largest such volcanic formation is Kazimura Cave in Hawaii, which is over seven miles (11 km) long.

**Figure 36
STALACTITES AND STALAGMITES:** Small streams of water leaking from the top of caves lead to a buildup of deposited minerals, forming these structures.

HOW DO GLACIERS MOVE?

IN SEVERAL PLACES AROUND THE world, the ground is always covered with thick layers of ice and snow. Such regions lie above the *snow line*—the level above which precipitation always falls in frozen form rather than as rain. At the north and south poles, temperatures are so cold that the only form of precipitation is snow, even at sea level. Regions located south of the arctic and north of the antarctic have higher snow lines. The level for the Olympic Mountains in the state of Washington, which are positioned halfway between the north pole and the equator, is about 5,500 feet (1,650 m). Points near the equator, where the prevailing temperatures are always warm, have very high snow lines: Mount Kilimanjaro in East Africa, just a few degrees south of the equator, has a snow line of about 18,000 feet (5,400 m).

When the amount of snowfall in a particular location exceeds the level of water lost by melting and evaporation, layers of frozen precipitation build up. As new snow falls, underlying layers are compressed by more and more weight, the force of which converts snow into compact ice. Over long periods of time, huge ice packs can form that cover large areas. Antarctica, a land mass of 5 and a half million square miles (14.3 million square km), is completely embedded under ice that is over 15,000 feet (4,500 m) thick in some places.

When ice fields in mountainous regions get so large and heavy that gravity forces them to move along the ground, a glacier is created. Some glaciers travel more than 100 feet (30 m) in a single day, while others creep along at only six inches (15 cm) per year. The pace of glacial movement is influenced by several factors, including the slope of the underlying land, the prevailing temperature, and the size of the particular glacier.

As you can imagine, examining the movement of glaciers first hand is rather difficult because of their slow speed, remote locations, and the constant freezing weather in glacial regions. It is also dangerous work, since the shifting ice can crack open or collapse without warning. But enough information has been obtained to suggest that a combination of dynamic factors operate within a glacier to cause its movement. Let's now consider the forces that cause these huge ice packs to migrate across the land.

The massive weight of thousands of tons of packed ice in a glacier exerts tremendous force on the bottom layer in contact with the ground. This extreme pressure pushes the frozen water molecules close together. Although ice has a solid structure, the individual molecules within it still display some movement, and when they are pressed closely together, they collide more frequently. Such collisions raise the energy level of water molecules, which makes them move faster and lose their rigid connections with each other. The result is that the bottom ice begins to melt, forming a thin layer of water between the glacier and the earth. This fluid lubricates the two surfaces and allows the glacier to slide along the ground as diagrammed in Figure 37.

This sliding action is not the only way glaciers move along. The middle regions of ice are also under heavy pressure, though not enough to produce melting. Within this central area, layers of ice respond to gravitational pull by sliding over one another, much like a deck of cards that fans out when tilted (Figure 37). Overall, this gives the glacier a somewhat elastic consistency, allowing it to mold and conform to the underlying terrain. The result is that glacial flow proceeds down a mountainside the way thick syrup spreads along a surface, with the middle region actually moving faster than the top layer. This gives many glaciers the appearance of frozen rivers slowly winding their way through a mountain pass.

During the earth's long history, there have been several *ice ages*—long periods of very cold conditions that allowed glaciers to extend over a large portion of the earth's surface. The most recent ice age ended about 10,000 years ago; before that, glaciers extended far enough south to cover the northern plain states of the United States. The work of ancient glaciers can be seen in many parts of the world today. As these huge ice packs receded, they left deep mountain valleys and sharp dividing ridges, the result of millions of years of geologic sculpturing by mighty glaciers.

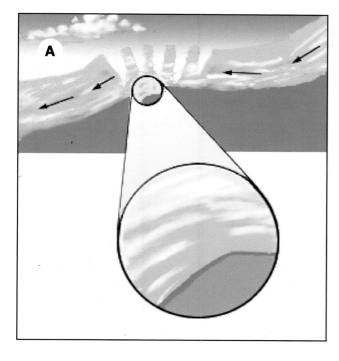

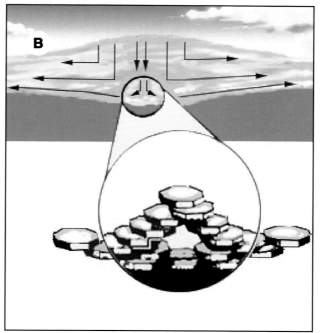

**Figure 37
CAUSES OF GLACIAL MOVEMENT:** (A) Pressure from the heavy weight of a glacier melts ice next to the ground, providing lubrication and allowing movement. (B) Ice crystals are somewhat "plastic" and can slide over one another when pressure is intense.

Glacial ice formations, opposite, Mt. Rainier, Washington. Columbia Tidewater glacier, below, Prince William Sound, Alaska.

WHERE DO ICEBERGS COME FROM?

Iᴄᴇʙᴇʀɢꜱ ᴀʀᴇ ᴀ ᴍᴀᴊᴇꜱᴛɪᴄ ᴘʜᴇɴᴏᴍᴇɴᴏɴ few of us ever get to see in person. They are blocks of freshwater ice floating in the ocean and they can be very large: In 1956, a single body of ice covering nearly 12,500 square miles (32,500 sq km) was discovered floating free in ocean waters. Icebergs are found almost exclusively in the two polar regions—a detail that provides a clue about how they are formed.

Those regions of the world that are encased in glacial ice, such as Antarctica and most of Greenland, exhibit a general current of ice pushing outward in all directions from a center point. As glaciers move this icy mass across the land, which is usually curved and bumpy, stress creates large cracks in the ice called *crevasses*. By the time a section of ice has journeyed across the land mass and reached the seashore, it can be fractured and divided into separate blocks. As the glacier continues to push these blocks outward, they break off completely from the glacier and fall into the sea, a process known as *calving*, which marks the birth of an iceberg (Figure 38).

If minimal fracturing has occurred in a glacial flow that reaches the shore, it can extend out over the ocean to form an *ice shelf*. The shelf is then eroded and stressed from underneath by ocean currents, tides, and waves until the outer shelf cracks off and splashes into the sea.

One might think that the hard, compact nature of icebergs along with their heavy weight—usually millions of tons would make them sink, but they don't because the density of ice is lower than the density of water. In general, solids are more dense than liquids, because the molecules in a solid are packed together very tightly, while liquid substances exhibit a looser, more open structure. But H_2O is an exception to the rule. The unique properties of water molecules cause them to align in a rather open crystalline structure when they freeze into a solid phase, leaving spaces in between. Thus a square inch (or square centimeter) of ice has fewer total water molecules in it than a square inch (or square centimeter) of liquid water, which means that ice has a lower density. This is why ice floats.

The density of ice is only slightly lower than the density of water, which causes icebergs to be partially submerged below the water line. Only about one-eighth of the total mass floats above the water, with the rest underneath and out of view. This is why icebergs can be very dangerous when they migrate into shipping lanes. For the most part, icebergs are confined to the polar regions of the globe, but occasionally they move farther out, migrating beyond the fiftieth parallel in both hemispheres. This occurs when storms stir up normal currents and carry icebergs toward the equator.

Once in the water, icebergs gradually melt and evaporate, returning their fresh water to liquid and gaseous forms to be recycled through the earth's circulating water system as illustrated in Figure 38. Typically, this takes only a few weeks for icebergs that move into warmer waters, whereas a very large one that stays in cold ocean currents can last several years.

Figure 38
PRODUCTION OF ICEBERGS: As glaciers flow into the ocean, chunks of ice break off to form icebergs.

WHY ARE THERE EARTHQUAKES?

THE EARTH'S OUTER CRUST IS a constantly changing structure that moves and reshapes the land around us. Because this process is incredibly slow, measured in millions of years, we are usually unaware of it. But occasionally a sudden and violent shift in the land occurs that vibrates and shakes the ground beneath our feet. These rapid large-scale movements, known as earthquakes, do indeed capture our attention and make us more aware of the dynamic nature of our planet.

Until about thirty years ago, geologists did not have a clear picture of why the earth's surface is in a state of continuous flux. Explanations centered around the large-scale erosion that moves millions of tons of dirt and rock from one location to another around the globe. It was thought that the gradual loss of large masses of material in high-erosion areas resulted in a general uplift of the land, while low-lying regions and ocean bottoms where eroded matter is deposited sank under the increased weight. Thus, sections of the earth's surface might fall and rise as overlying land is stripped away or piled up over long periods of time.

A similar phenomenon is in fact caused by the action of glaciers. The heavy weight of ice fields can push underlying land downward, sometimes as much as 2,000 feet (600 m). When such glaciers melt and recede, a process that takes thousands of years, the land slowly lifts back up to its original level.

These "weight distribution" forces probably do contribute to movement of the earth's crust, but they do not fully explain the observed patterns. It was not until 1960, when geologists developed a unifying theory known as *plate tectonics*, that we began to understand how and why the earth's surface moves. The heart of this idea is that the outer surface of the earth's crust—the *lithosphere*—is continuously replenished with the underlying *asthenosphere*, which is composed of softer, molten material. Convection within the asthenosphere causes magma to move in currents, which in turn drives movement of the overlying crust.

The cycle begins when magma from the interior pushes up and hardens along specific cracks in the surface called *ridges*. For the most part, these ridges lie deep in the oceans between continents. The buildup of the ocean floor along ridges is accompanied by the lithosphere moving outward. Since the outer "skin" of the earth is rigid, it cannot move as a single unit but is broken into pieces called *plates*. The seven major plates are shown in Figure 39. Plates move away from ridge areas at an average rate of a few inches (or centimeters) per year.

Eventually the various plates are forced against each other because of expansion in ridge areas. The interface between the edges of two plates is called a *fault,* and it is here that the movement of opposing plates is most apparent.

When one plate is pushing against another, something has to give. Often this conflict is resolved by one of the plates sliding underneath the other. In this way, the lithosphere is returned to the asthenosphere where it is melted and recycled. This process can elevate the margin of the upper plate to lift up new terrain or form deep ocean trenches where the lower plate is forced downward.

In some cases, two plates meet head on and are both forced upward. An example is the junction between the Indian-Australian Plate and Eurasian Plate, where the tremendous pressure of these colliding masses has pushed up the Himalayas. Plates can also slide laterally past each other to relieve pressure. The San Andreas Fault that runs through the western edge of California is the result of the Pacific Plate sliding laterally against the North American Plate.

The fault lines created by adjacent plates are the margin where built-up tension from shifting land masses is resolved. Edges between plates do not usually slide smoothly past each other, rather their rough dry surfaces often catch and prevent gradual movement. This leads to a buildup of pressure that bends rock layers, creating bulges and curves in surrounding formations (Figure 40). When the forces responsible for creating the pressure become greater than the frictional resistance and strength of the rock formation, something snaps. The two plates scrape quickly along the fault line, sending vibrations that shake the ground for many miles (or kilometers) around. This event, known as an earthquake, relieves the built-up pressure—though only temporarily. Further plate movement again creates tension, priming the fault for another quake.

Seismologists, scientists who focus their research on earthquakes, have a number of ways to measure and study these phenomena. The most common means of reporting seismic events is the *Richter scale*, which assigns a value to earthquakes according to their overall energy release. This is not a linear scale—an earthquake measuring 5.5 on this scale is about thirty times stronger than an earthquake measuring 4.5. An earthquake with a magnitude of 3 can be felt out to about 20 miles (32 km) from the point where the quake originates. There are approximately 150,000 tremors of this size on the earth every year. A magnitude of 5 accompanies medium-strength quakes, which can be felt 190 miles (304 km) away from their center and occur about 1,500 times each year. The largest earthquakes, with shock waves that travel over 750 miles (1,200 km) out, measure above 8 on the Richter scale and are rare, occurring about once a year on the average.

Accurately predicting earthquakes is a goal seismologists are working toward. A feature that is monitored and studied is the frequency of earthquakes along lateral faults. A long period of inactivity along the border between adjacent plates may indicate a buildup of tension. One such region is along the San Andreas Fault; its relative silence for many years has led to speculation that this region is due for a major quake.

Not enough is yet known to accurately guess when earthquakes will occur or exactly how large they will be. But by recording and analyzing seismic events, scientists hope to someday be able to predict major earthquakes and forewarn inhabitants in threatened locations.

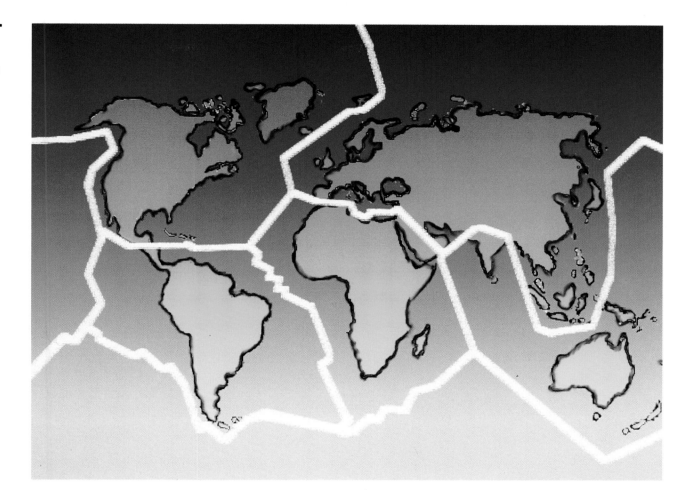

Figure 39
MAJOR TECTONIC PLATES (right): Cracks in the earth's crust divide the surface into several major pieces known as "plates," shown here by the solid lines.

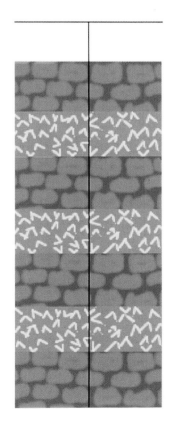

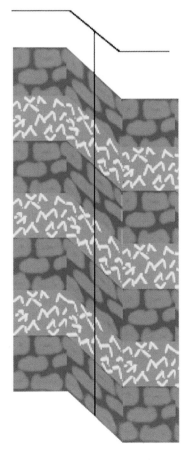

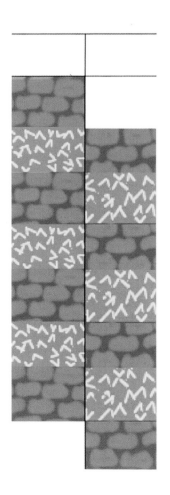

A

B

C

Figure 40
FAULT LINE (left): The surfaces between adjoining plates are sites of extreme pressure buildup, which eventually produces rapid movement to relieve pressure. This movement is called an earthquake.

Dave Bartruff/FPG International

The earthquake that hit San Francisco, above and right, in 1989 caused extensive damage, including the collapse of large sections of freeways. Left: The San Andreas Fault, Carrizo Plain, California.

© Larry Grant/FPG International

WHAT IS A VOLCANO?

MOST OF THE EARTH'S INTERIOR consists of very hot molten rock, some portions of which reach temperatures of 7,000°F (3,900°C). Fortunately for us, this heated inner region is sealed in by a much cooler solid crust. But in certain locations around the world, material from within the interior escapes to the surface. When this happens, liquid magma spews out onto the surface and cools, building a cone-shaped structure called a volcano.

Various parts of the world have experienced volcanic activity throughout history. Currently, there are about 600 active volcanoes on our planet. These do not occur randomly over the face of the earth but are confined almost exclusively to very narrow belts in specific areas. Most of these active volcanoes lie in a circular loop around the edge of the Pacific Ocean, forming a "ring of fire" along the coasts of the enclosing continents (Figure 41). A comparison of points of volcanic activity (Figure 41) with the earth's major geologic plates (Figure 39 in the previous section) reveals that volcanoes are restricted almost entirely to the margins between certain adjacent plates. In particular, the "ring of fire" lies almost exactly over the perimeter of the Pacific Plate. Let's now consider the forces that operate in these zones to produce volcanoes.

The type of plate junction most suited to volcano formation is a *subduction zone*—where one plate slides underneath another. On most of its borders, the Pacific Plate is sliding under surrounding continental plates. This process creates heat and pressure that partially melts the bottom region of the overlying plate as well as part of the descending plate. The result is the production of magma, which sometimes finds a path back up to the surface and forms a volcano. Oceanic ridges are also sites of volcanic activity, where magma pushes up between separating plates and flows out onto the ocean floor.

In a few locations, volcanoes occur within plates. These are thought to be caused by localized "hot spots" where unusually hot magma pushes up underneath the earth's crust. The best guess about the source of these hot spots is that they are plumes of magma rising from deep in the earth's interior, where the temperature is much hotter than higher zones. These superheated pockets of magma bypass the normal circulation pattern of the interior and push upward against the overlying crust, sometimes breaking through. The Hawaiian Islands are a group of volcanoes that were formed in this way. As the earth's crust moves over this hot spot, magma

**Figure 41
AREAS OF
VOLCANIC ACTIVITY**
(right): The locations
of the earth's active
volcanoes are shown in
red. Note that almost
all volcanoes are posi-
tioned along the edges
of tectonic plates.

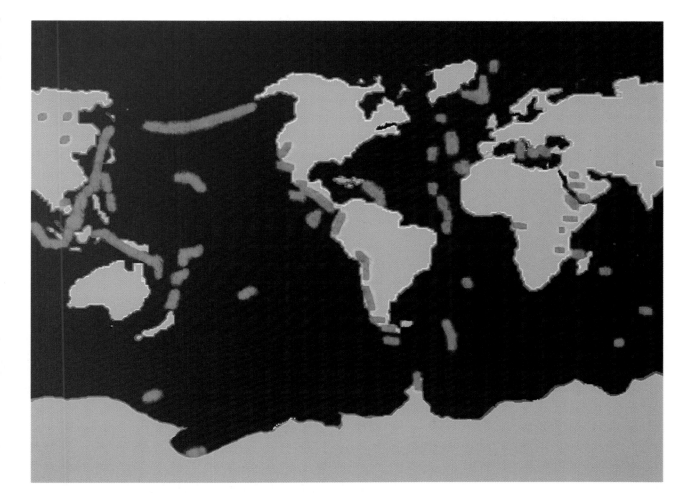

occasionally finds an outlet and forms a volcano, which becomes an island. As the ocean floor slides along, the most recently formed island moves past the hot spot. Eventually another eruption occurs, creating yet another island. This is why the Hawaiian Islands are strung out in a line, as if marching northwest across the ocean as the Pacific Plate moves along over the region of very hot magma.

When magma does find passage to the surface, it can erupt in several different ways. If the channel is fairly wide and not impinged, liquid rock bubbles up slowly and flows smoothly out over the cone in a continuous pattern. This mild type of eruption is typical in ridge areas and in hot spot regions such as the Hawaiian Islands.

An important factor that can influence the magnitude of the eruption event is high levels of dissolved gases in the magma, especially steam. Under the high pressure environment inside the earth, gases within the magma are compressed and stay dissolved in the surrounding matter. But as magma approaches the surface, gases within the channel expand rapidly with explosive force, greatly amplifying the eruption.

If a volcano's main channel is narrow and contains loose rocks and debris, magma can become temporarily trapped and build up pressure until sufficient force blasts the plug upward. The most violent eruptions are caused by such conditions. One of the largest explosions in recorded history occurred in 1883 when the volcanic island of Krakatoa in Indonesia blew up, sending several cubic miles (or cubic kilometers) of dust into the air that traveled completely around the globe.

More recently, Mount Saint Helens in the state of Washington blew its top. In early 1980, observers watched for several weeks as a giant dome swelled over the mouth of this volcano, indicative of a blocked magma chamber building up pressure. On May 18, part of the mountain gave way and slid downward, exposing the highly pressurized magma chamber that exploded outward with tremendous force. The blast completely devastated a 200-square-mile (520 sq km) area and caused shock waves that knocked down huge trees twenty miles (32 km) away. Even today, more than ten years later, large sections near the crater have not recovered, providing a stark reminder of the forces at work deep within our planet.

When superheated lava from a volcano reaches the ocean, powerful explosions occur, left, that hurl rock and steam into the air. The upper portion of a volcano, right, frequently takes the shape of a crater.

WHERE DOES OIL COME FROM?

THE GEOLOGIC PROCESSES THAT FORM oil are important because modern civilization depends heavily on this substance as a source of gasoline, natural gas, and heating oil. *Petroleum,* the technical name for crude oil straight from the ground, is also the starting material for hundreds of other products including plastics, synthetic fabrics, dyes, asphalt, and even medicines. The formation of oil deposits is an interesting phenomenon by itself, which is why we will now briefly consider the series of events leading to the creation of oil within the earth.

Oil is formed in ocean basins—large shallow depressions—where huge amounts of plant and animal matter build up. As these living organisms die and settle on the ocean floor, they are covered with sedimentary layers, such as sand and clay, which are carried into the basin from eroding land masses. Over long periods of time, these layers of *organic* matter—the remnants of dead plants and animals—along with sedimentary material, build up to form thick rock formations.

All living organisms are made up of complex molecules containing carbon, hydrogen, oxygen, nitrogen, sulfur, and traces of many other elements. Trapped within the sedimentary rock, organic remains decompose into simpler molecular arrangements. This is caused by microscopic organisms such as bacteria and also by the heat and pressure of the surrounding rock. The chemical reactions that take place separate oxygen, nitrogen, and sulfur from the carbon and hydrogen, leaving chains of carbon atoms with hydrogen atoms attached. These chains of carbons with their associated hydrogens are called *hydrocarbons* and are the major constituent of crude oil, accounting for up to 98 percent of the total volume.

The chemical and physical properties of hydrocarbons are a function of the length of the carbon chain (Figure 42). Very short chains, containing four or less carbons, exist as gases such as methane, propane, and butane. If a chain has from five to twenty carbons, it exists in a liquid state. An example is octane, eight carbons long, which is a component of gasoline. Hydrocarbons that are longer than twenty carbons are solids. Paraffin wax is a mixture of hydrocarbon chains ranging from twenty-two to thirty carbons in length.

All different lengths of hydrocarbons form within tiny crevices throughout sedimentary layers. Subsequently they can migrate and collect into porous layers of rock such as sandstone. Oil is usually carried to such reservoirs by water. But since oil has a lower density than water, it tends to float and thus accumulates above the waterline. If an opening to the surface exists, oil can flow out onto the ocean bottom to form a sticky layer that has a consistency of pitch or asphalt. When oil leaks out onto dry land, the lighter elements evaporate, while the heavy components thicken and form tar pits.

When hard, impermeable rock covers a region where oil is collecting, the hydrocarbons build up to form large underground pockets of crude oil (Figure 43). The lighter gaseous hydrocarbons sift to the upper portion, the liquid oil pools below, and a water layer is often found beneath. It is these pockets of accumulated oil and gas that are tapped and refined into various petroleum products.

The formation of an oil field is an incredibly long process, taking as many as one million years to fully develop. Only a small fraction of all the oil created in oceanic basins makes its way into large underground pools. It is estimated that 99 percent of all the oil formed remains tightly trapped within rock and does not coalesce into porous strata where it can be easily recovered. Researchers are now exploring economic methods of extracting oil from such rocks.

The process of oil formation continues today in large ocean basins such as the Gulf of Mexico and the Persian Gulf, but this is a very slow process that will not be complete for many hundreds of generations. Currently, the world's oil reserves are being used up much faster than new deposits are being formed—a fact that has stimulated research into alternative energy sources.

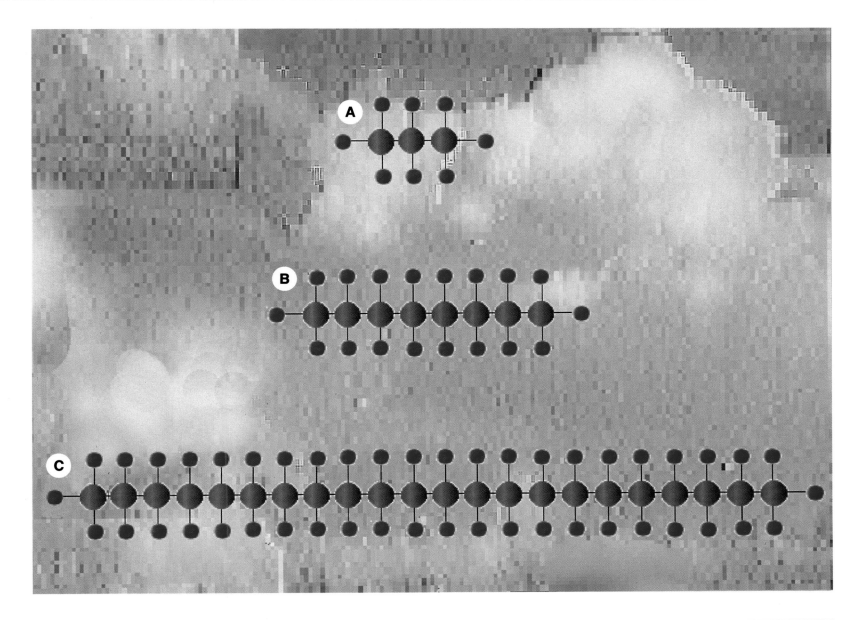

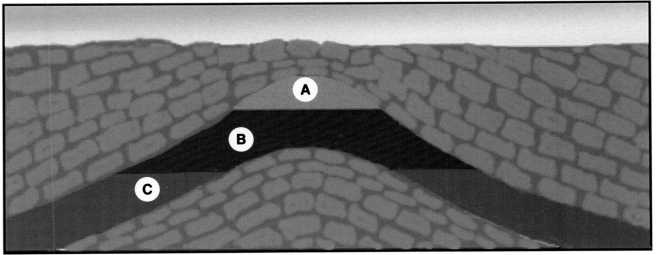

**Figures 42 and 43
MOLECULAR
STRUCTURE OF
HYDROCARBONS**
(above, Figure 42):
A) Propane, a gas;
B) octane, a liquid;
C) component of
paraffin, a solid.
**FORMATION OF
OIL POCKET**
(right, Figure 43):
A) Lighter gases
trapped at top; B) oil
layer; C) heavier water
layer beneath.

PLANT LIFE

WHY DO SEEDLINGS ALWAYS GROW UP?

AMONG THE MANY WONDERS OF nature, the most intriguing of all is life. Even the simplest living organisms, such as microscopic bacteria, are sophisticated chemical factories that generate thousands of complex reactions every second. Despite the enormous variety and complexity of life, just a handful of atomic building blocks account for over 99 percent of the physical composition of all life forms. These main ingredients are carbon, hydrogen, oxygen, and nitrogen. You may recognize these names: All of these elements are found in abundance in the inanimate world. What makes living things unique is the remarkable way in which these four elements are joined and organized into very large, complex molecules that can carry out special functions.

Biologists group all living things into three categories: the *animal kingdom,* the *plant kingdom,* and a special classification termed *Protista* for the many types of microscopic organisms— such as bacteria and yeast—that exist as single-celled forms. In the final sections of this book, we will briefly examine a few representative features of just one of these groups: plants. A discussion of selected characteristics of plant life will yield insights about living organisms in general. Let's begin with a particularly interesting feature of growing plants—their ability to spatially orient their stems and roots.

Most plants start out as seeds. When a seed germinates, two distinct structures emerge—the root and the stem. In a bed of sprouting seedlings, a noticeable feature is the uniform direction of growth of these two primary parts. A quick inspection finds all the stems pointed upward, and pulling up a few plants reveals that the main roots are always directed straight down into the soil. This is obviously beneficial since roots function only underground, while leaves that will emerge from the stem later must be exposed to sunlight in order to survive and function. But how does a young plant accomplish this crucial orientation?

Before scientists discovered the mechanism that causes this phenomenon, a number of explanations seemed feasible. For example, it seemed possible that the sun-warmed dirt above the sprouting seed might attract the stem structure up toward the surface. Alternatively, the seedling might respond to gravitational forces and orient growth accordingly so that stems grow against that force and roots grow toward it. Still another option might be that seedlings *don't* always grow up: Perhaps a collection of seedlings grows in all directions randomly, and only those stems that happen to grow upward and break through the soil survive and continue.

To determine which, if any, of these hypotheses is correct, a scientist would design and carry out experiments to narrow down the choices. For example, careful excavation of the soil at an early stage of germination would reveal whether or not seedlings grow in random directions. And sprouting seeds in a dark room would show if light or heat is a source of attraction for the young stem structure.

Such experiments would prove to be negative for these two hypotheses—all seedlings in the soil send stems up and roots down, and this occurs in the absence of light or heat from a specific direction. By default then, gravity would be implicated as the force that aligns plant growth in a vertical direction.

But a good scientist would not be satisfied with this indirect conclusion. To confirm that gravity is indeed the causative force, a more definitive experiment would be needed. Just such an experiment was carried out some 180 years ago by an English scientist named Thomas Knight. He attached potted seedlings to a spinning wheel as shown in Figure 45. The wheel was then rotated while the seedlings grew. The wheel's motion created centrifugal force in a horizontal plane—as if gravity was pulling sideways instead of vertically. This caused the plants to align their stems and roots horizontally along the direction of force, demonstrating conclusively that gravity is the force responsible for the direction of stem and root growth. This directional growth in response to gravity is called *geotropism.*

Further experiments have detailed how geotropism is regulated in growing plants. Within the cells of the plant's growing stem and root are specialized starch granules called *statoliths.* Gravity pulls these granules to the bottom of cells, where they stimulate the production of growth hormones. To understand how this occurs, let's consider what happens when a young plant is bent laterally as shown in Figure 44. The change of position causes the statoliths to realign on what was the side of the cells but is now the bottom. Hormone production is increased, and growth occurs most rapidly in the cells on the lower side of the stem. The faster growing bottom side forces the stem to bend in an upward direction. As the stem achieves a more and more vertical orientation, the statoliths reposition, maintaining an upright position as the plant continues to grow.

In the root, the site of statolith-directed hormone action is reversed. Thus if a root is repositioned horizontally, the repositioned statoliths direct increased growth in cells on the *top* side of the root, bending the root back down into the soil. By this mechanism, plants can realign their growth, which gives them the best chance of surviving.

Once a plant has passed the seedling stage and matures, light becomes an important source for directional growth and also a requirement for sustained growth and proliferation. But in the earliest stages of plant development, gravity alone orients the stem and roots in their respective optimal directions.

Figure 44
By the mechanism of *geotropism*, plants that are knocked over can adjust new growth in an upward direction, allowing them to survive.

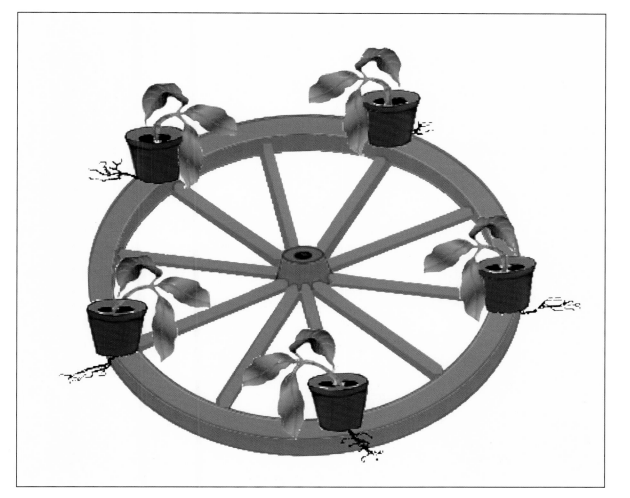

Figure 45
If plants are rotated on a wheel, they will orient leaves and roots laterally, along the lines of force, demonstrating that gravity is the key determinant of the direction of plant growth.

HOW DO PLANTS GET WATER UP TO THEIR LEAVES?

ALL PLANTS ARE TOTALLY dependent on water for growth and reproduction. In fact, water is the factor that triggers a dormant seed into germination and subsequent transformation into an active plant. Water is the solvent in which complex biochemical molecules within cells are dissolved, allowing them to interact and perform their specialized functions. H_2O molecules are also vital intermediates and products of several chemical reactions that typify living systems. In addition, water is the medium in which important nutrients and minerals are transported to all parts of a growing plant.

Because water is so essential, plants contain a network of tubular cells and vessels that serve to carry water to every part. The cells within the root of a plant are specially designed to absorb water from the surrounding soil. Once inside the plant, water molecules collect in a type of plant tissue called *xylem*, which carries water and dissolved minerals upward through the stem to the leaves. There is also a separate kind of tissue called *phloem* for transporting nutrients from the leaves down to the rest of the plant.

This cellular plumbing system allows continuous movement of water from the roots up to the leaves. And remarkably, this flow occurs against the force of gravity, without any kind of pumping mechanism to force the flow upward and without any energy expenditure. How does a plant manage this feat?

A key to understanding this phenomenon is a close examination of a plant's leaves. The surface of a leaf contains tiny openings called *stomata*. Through these structures, plants absorb carbon dioxide (an important process we will consider later). Stomata also allow water in the leaves to escape into the atmosphere, a process called *transpiration*. It is this process of water loss through stomata into the atmosphere that is responsible for the upward movement of water through plants. Let's now consider the details of this remarkable process.

The air in contact with leaf surfaces has a very high capacity to absorb moisture. This absorption of water provides the energy that drives the system of upward flow. As water molecules are absorbed out of the stomata into the air, they pull more water molecules along behind them. This is possible because of the cohesive properties of water—the individual molecules exhibit strong attraction for each other and tend to "hang on" together. Thus, a chain of water molecules are pulled upward through the length of the plant (Figure 46).

The ability of a column of water to be pulled upward without collapsing is influenced by the column's width. The narrower the channel, the higher water can rise before the molecules separate and fall back down. Within plants, the extremely narrow tubular xylem allows pressure to build to many thousands of pounds per square inch (kilograms per square centimeter) without the individual molecules pulling apart. This pressure can pull water upward to amazing heights—some giant redwood trees sponsor leafy growth nearly 350 feet (105 m) above the ground.

Thus it is the process of transpiration, pulling thin columns of cohesive water molecules up the stems of plants, that is responsible for transporting water from the bottom roots of plants up to their leaves.

**Figure 46
MECHANISM OF WATER FLOW IN PLANTS:** The cohesive nature of water molecules allows them to be pulled upward in thin columns within specialized tissues of plants.

HOW DO PLANTS MAKE OXYGEN?

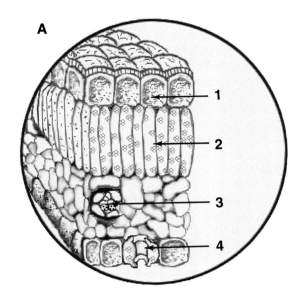

ALL FORMS OF ANIMAL LIFE require oxygen to survive. Without this vital gas, we would perish in a matter of minutes. Fortunately, oxygen is abundant in our atmosphere—but only because it is constantly replenished by the world's plant population. Active plants put out an incredible amount of oxygen. Under optimal conditions, green algae, for example, produce thirty times their own volume in oxygen every hour. Let's examine the process by which plants manufacture this essential gas.

Plants possess the remarkable ability to convert solar radiation into stored chemical energy. This process, called *photosynthesis,* is the fundamental reaction that supports life on the earth. All of our common fuels such as wood, coal, and petroleum originated with this reaction. The vegetables and fruits that make up our diet are produced by photosynthesis, and even dairy and meat products come from animals that feed on plants and thus are indirectly produced by this same basic process.

Photosynthesis is described by the following equation:

$$6\ H_2O + 6\ CO_2 + \text{light energy} \xrightarrow[\text{enzymes}]{\text{chlorophyll}} C_6H_{12}O_6 + 6\ O_2$$

This represents the input of six water molecules (H_2O) that enter from the roots, plus six molecules of carbon dioxide gas (CO_2) that enter the leaves from the air. In the presence of light, special molecules called *chlorophylls* and *enzymes* convert these two compounds into sugar ($C_6H_{12}O_6$) and release six molecules of oxygen (O_2) as a by-product. As a result, oxygen is provided for animals, which in turn give off carbon

dioxide as a by-product—one of the compounds required by plants. Thus plants and animals are locked in a dependent relationship, each producing chemicals required by the other.

The process of photosynthesis begins when light from the sun enters the leaves of a plant. Within leaf cells are special structures called *chloroplasts* (see Figure 47a). Inside chloroplasts are layers of membranes called *grana* that contain *chlorophyll* molecules. Chlorophyll exhibits a very special property: It can absorb light energy. When it does, electrons associated with the chlorophyll molecule are raised to a higher energy state. These energized electrons are then passed along a chain of neighboring chlorophyll molecules, and the electrons release a small amount of energy at each step. This energy from the passing electrons is captured in intermediate chemicals that are later used to produce sugars. These sugars represent the final stored form of energy in the cycle.

The oxygen produced by photosynthesis comes from water. As part of the reaction, the two hydrogens are dissociated from water, leaving just oxygen, which is given off as a gas. The hydrogen atoms are eventually attached to carbon dioxide to build sugar molecules.

The amount of organic matter produced by photosynthesis on a global scale is truly phenomenal. Scientists estimate this total by measuring the increase in mass of small sections of plant habitats such as oceans, forests, and open prairies. With this information and approximations of the globe's coverage by various plant types, it is possible to estimate that every year 100 billion tons (90 billion metric tons) of carbon are transferred from inorganic forms such as carbon dioxide into organic materials such as sugars and more complex biochemical molecules.

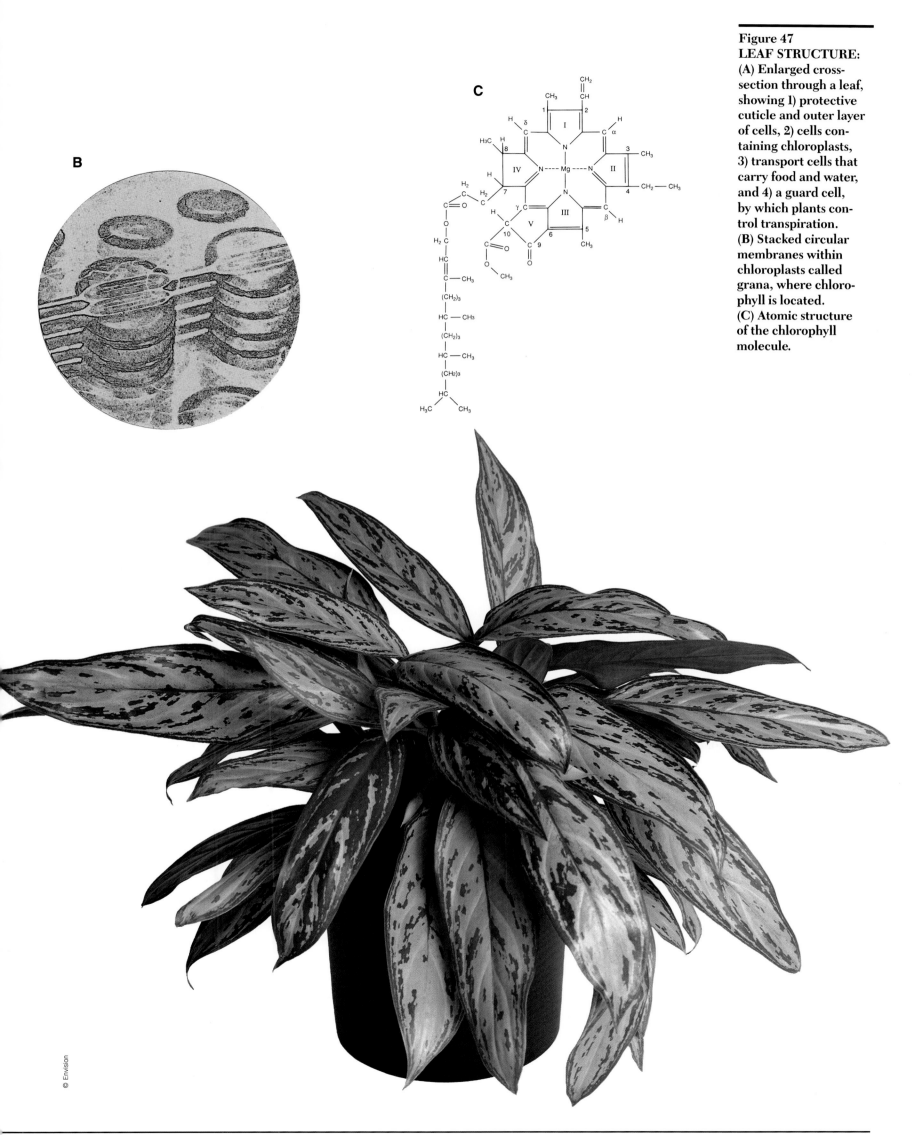

B

C

Figure 47
LEAF STRUCTURE:
(A) Enlarged cross-section through a leaf, showing 1) protective cuticle and outer layer of cells, 2) cells containing chloroplasts, 3) transport cells that carry food and water, and 4) a guard cell, by which plants control transpiration.
(B) Stacked circular membranes within chloroplasts called grana, where chlorophyll is located.
(C) Atomic structure of the chlorophyll molecule.

HOW DO PLANTS SURVIVE IN THE DESERT?

A HALLMARK OF LIVING ORGANISMS is their capacity to adapt to the environment in which they reside. Over very long periods of time natural selection molds species to better fit their surroundings. After millions of years of evolution, many current life forms possess highly specialized features that help them survive, even under very harsh conditions. As an example of adaptation, let's consider how plants are able to live in the demanding environment of the world's deserts.

In several ways, deserts are well suited for sponsoring plant life. The abundant sunshine provides nearly constant light for photosynthesis—the reaction that produces chemical energy for the plant's activities—and the daily heat that is typical in desert areas is ideal for plant growth, since the chemical processes within plant cells operate maximally at relatively high temperatures. In addition, the soil in many desert regions is actually quite fertile and can provide a rich nutrient base for plant growth. But all of these features cannot overcome the major deficiency inherent in desert environments: extremely limited amounts of water.

Because water is essential for plants to flourish, the adaptations displayed by desert species have a common theme in preserving this vital compound. They accomplish this by special anatomical features designed to absorb and retain whatever precious water is available. Thus, plants that have successfully colonized arid regions look quite different from those growing in lush tropical areas.

For example, desert plants typically have smaller and fewer leaves. Some species, particularly various types of cacti, do not have leaves at all. Leaves contain openings called stomata that allow *transpiration*—the evaporation of water into the air. This process is the force that transports water and dissolved nutrients and minerals up through the plant. But transpiration results in extensive water loss, a luxury desert plants cannot afford. The absence of true leaves on cacti reduces their total surface area, which means there is less opportunity for water loss by evaporation. In addition, the outer surface or *cuticle* of such plants is covered with a waxy substance that further reduces evaporation. Also, what few stomata cacti *do* have are shut tightly during the hot daytime hours, reducing transpiration.

These adaptations are not without cost. Tightly closed stomata present a serious problem—it prevents intake of carbon dioxide from the air, which is a necessary component in the chemical reactions that produce energy-rich compounds. Desert plants circumvent this dilemma by opening their stomata at night, when less evaporation occurs because the air is cooler. This allows influx of carbon dioxide, but not at quite the right time. Ordinarily CO_2 is required during the day, when photosynthesis generates the energy required to build carbon dioxide molecules into sugars. But desert species have another adaptation to deal with this problem. The CO_2 taken in during the night is converted into *malic acid* and stored until daylight. Then the malic acid is broken back down into carbon dioxide and shuttled into the sugar-building pathway.

In this way, cacti can minimize water loss by day and still obtain necessary gases from the air by night. The adaptations that maintain carbon dioxide levels and reduce transpiration lead to less efficient energy production and reduced growth rate, but this is a trade-off desert plants can live with, so to speak.

© Fritz Polking/Dembinsky Photo Association

The root systems of desert plants are designed to capture the maximum amount of water. They are typically very thin and profuse, extending long distances away from the plant body. Most of these roots lie just under the surface of the ground. This allows rapid absorption of water when precipitation does occur, even if it does not penetrate very deep into the soil.

When a rare storm brings rainfall to the desert, plants take full advantage of it. The tissues of cacti in particular are designed to swell up with water when the opportunity arises, building an internal store that is then available during long dry spells.

Another strategy employed by some species that live in arid regions is to simply avoid the dry conditions altogether. An example is the California golden poppy, which does not have any special adaptations for survival in dry climates. Instead it remains as a dormant seed until adequate rainfall activates germination. Once this occurs, the plant develops quickly, blooms, and forms new seeds all in a matter of a few weeks. By the time the plant begins to die, the seeds are mature and

ready to lie dormant for several more years if necessary until another rainfall of sufficient magnitude restarts the cycle.

The special adaptations displayed by desert plants are examples of compromise. Plants such as cacti tend to be rugged, inefficient, slow-growing, and not very glamorous, and wild flowers such as desert poppies, though lovely in their season, rush through their entire life cycle in just a few weeks. But such species are able to inhabit the driest locations on earth, where other more elegant species would quickly wither and perish. In the biological world, characteristics such as beauty, economy, and even lengthy survival of individual organisms are expendable if it is necessary to achieve the primary goal: survival of the species.

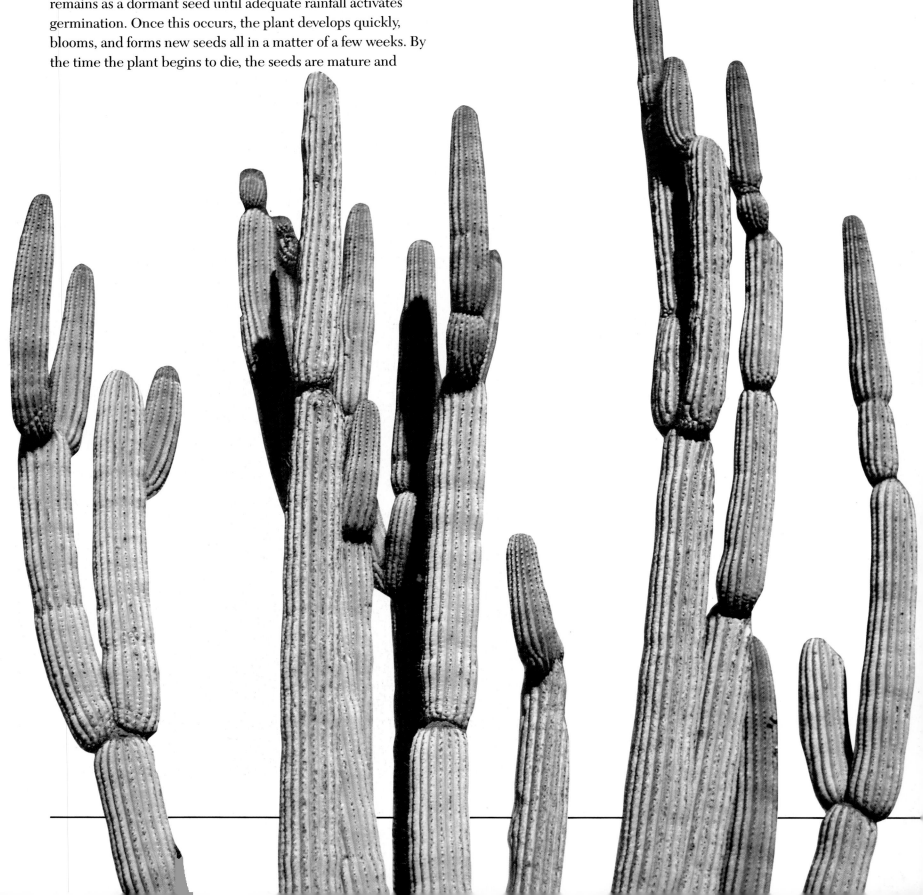

WHY ARE FLOWERS PRETTY?

© John Shaw/Tom Stack & Associates

OF ALL THE CHARACTERISTICS OF living organisms, the most remarkable is the ability to reproduce. A large portion of the resources of every kind of plant and animal is expended on this most important of all biological mandates—the perpetuation of the species. Most plants reproduce by the mechanism known as *sexual reproduction*. This involves the mixing of the genetic material from two distinct structures, one female and one male, which are often both contained in a single plant. In this way, the genes of a particular species are shuffled and recombined, so that the offspring manifests physical characteristics of the parents and sometimes brand-new traits of its own. Thus, sexual reproduction creates diversity in a community of similar organisms, which allows the species as a whole to adapt to change and evolve over time.

Because plants remain fixed in one spot throughout their life cycle, sexual reproduction is a particular challenge. Their immobility prevents direct contact to combine *gametes*—the reproductive cells—even though a single plant usually contains both types. There are, however, alternative strategies. Since they cannot effectively transfer gametes themselves, plants use a technique we are all familiar with: They entice others to do the work for them.

Most plants produce flowers as part of their reproductive cycle. Within the flowers are male structures called *pollen*, which contain *sperm*, the male gametes, and also female gametes called *ovaries*. The pollen grains develop at the ends of thin projections called *stamens*, while the ovaries are maintained within a protective tube called the *pistil*, where pollen must be deposited to effect fertilization. Some varieties of flowers also produce *nectar*, a nutrient-rich substance, and still others emit strong fragrances.

Flowers, pollen, nectar, and perfume-like odors all serve as attractants for insects and birds. When animals are lured to a flower by these inducements, they brush against the pollen, which is moist and sticky. Some of the pollen sticks to the visitor and is deposited on the pistil of another flower as the insect or bird moves from flower to flower.

This relationship between different life forms is called *symbiosis* and is a common theme in the living world. The symbiotic relationships between flowering plants and their pollinating animal partners is mutually productive—plants are able to reproduce, and the pollinators obtain life-sustaining food. Thus, both parties are dependent on one another, and both benefit from the interaction.

Some flowers have evolved into highly specialized forms that attract specific pollinators. An example is the buttercup flower, which is pollinated by honey bees. Bees can detect three colors: blue, yellow, and ultraviolet. Buttercups appear totally yellow to us, but these flowers actually contain pigments that reflect in the ultraviolet range as well. A mixture of yellow and ultraviolet pigments forms a color called *bee purple*, which honey bees can see, as illustrated in Figure 48. The yellow petals of the buttercup form a general signal visible from long distances, and the smaller bee-purple pattern in the center directs the pollinator to home in on the pollen. The bees then collect the pollen and stuff it into special sacks on their back legs for transportation to the hive where it will serve as food. But as the bee hops from flower to flower, some of the pollen rubs off on the pistil, completing the transfer of gametes.

Even a brief survey of flower shapes and colors reveals a staggering degree of variety. This is a result of evolution, which has fine-tuned flower traits to better attract specific insects or birds. For example, the major pollinators in north temperate zones, honey bees, do not see red. There is a corresponding sparsity of true red flowers in these regions—the reddish hues are usually tones of pink. The few true red flowers also contain ultraviolet pigments or small amounts of blue pigments mixed in. Red flowers are much more common in tropical zones, where birds, which *can* see red, are the main pollinators.

Thus flowers serve as brightly colored beacons that attract insects and other animals to aid in the plant's reproductive cycle. This assures the survival of flowering plants from generation to generation—a fact that is sure to make all of the gardeners among us very happy.

Figure 48
BEE PURPLE (left):
Honey bees are able to
see ultraviolet light,
which is present as a
mixture with yellow in
some flowers.

WHY DO PLANTS MAKE FRUIT?

THE END RESULT OF PLANT reproduction is the formation of seeds. These dormant embryos are self-contained and need only soil, water, and warmth to germinate into a mature plant. But again the immobility of plant life presents a problem. If the seeds simply fall to the ground next to the parent and sprout, the area will quickly become crowded. Young seedlings will compete for space to receive sunlight and for nutrients and water from the ground.

To overcome this problem, plants have evolved many different methods of *seed dispersal*. Some types of plants, such as dandelions, form tiny seeds equipped with thin sails to catch the wind and travel long distances through the air. Other seeds like coconuts can float until they reach distant shores and sprout. Still others like cockleburs form rough, spiny surfaces that help the seed attach to passing animals and be carried for miles before falling off to colonize new regions.

© Thomas Kitchin/Tom Stack & Associates

The dandelion forms very light-weight seeds that can float on the wind to colonize new ground.

© Christopher C. Bain

An elaborate and very effective means of seed dispersal is the formation of fruit. The seeds of fruit-bearing plants are embedded in a thick coat of tasty, nutritious material that is eaten by animals. Most types of fruit remain in an unattractive condition until the seeds mature. Unripe fruit is green in color, has a very sour or bitter taste, and does not give off a sweet, pleasing aroma. This prevents early harvesting of the seeds before they are fully formed. Once the seeds are ready, the fruit changes color—often to red or another distinctive shade. This provides for easy detection by birds and other fruit-eating animals. In addition, the fruit becomes sweet and soft and emits attractive odors.

Seeds consumed along with the fruit often survive intact and are carried inside the animal to new locations. Passage through the digestive tract of an animal can actually be beneficial— it moistens and softens the hard outer shell of some seed types, so that when they are excreted they sprout readily. The droppings of many types of animals contain viable seeds that grow into new plants.

Birds in particular are responsible for transporting seeds across vast distances. Most land mammals display a rather limited range of travel, and the relatively quick passage of seeds through their bodies—usually just a few hours—precludes wide-scale dispersal. But creatures on the wing can distribute seeds to far away regions. This creates the opportunity for plants to set up new colonies in habitats where they did not previously exist. Of course, their success will depend upon the availability of suitable soil, water, and appropriate climatic conditions.

Seed dispersal by fruit-eating animals is yet another example of symbiosis between plants and animals. Both life forms benefit from the process and over time have come to rely on the other for survival. When we look closely at life on the planet, symbiotic relationships between various kinds of organisms appear to be the rule rather than the exception. The wise observer will note this interdependency and consider how our management of the environment impacts on *all* forms of life.

WHY DO LEAVES CHANGE COLOR?

THE AUTUMN SEASON IN TEMPERATE zones presents a spectacular display of color as many kinds of trees shed their leaves. Stands of maple, oak, elm, birch, poplar, and many other species seem to contain every possible shade of yellow, orange, and red. What is the mechanism that produces this beautiful scene?

All living organisms consist of tiny individual units called *cells*. Each cell is a self-contained entity that can carry on the functions of life such as growth, metabolism, and reproduction. The kinds of cells that make up a tiny fern and a giant redwood are remarkably similar in structure and size—the difference is that the huge redwood has many more cells.

In higher life forms, such as plants, the cells within an individual organism exist to carry on specific activities. Thus, some cells elongate into xylem and phloem tissues to transport water, while others develop into sperm and eggs for reproduction, and some others form into bark to protect the exterior trunk and branches. Such specialization benefits the plant as a whole by allowing it to carry out sophisticated functions that the individual cells could not accomplish on their own.

Because plants are a collection of many cells, the organism can survive the loss of some of its members. In fact, the sloughing off of particular parts of the plant is very useful for some species and occurs on a regular basis. A good example is the process of *abscission*—the annual shedding of leaves that occurs in deciduous trees.

Under optimal conditions when sunlight and water are plentiful, leaves are an essential component of these plants. Photosynthesis, the reaction that produces food for the rest of the tree, occurs within the leaves. Leaves are also the location of stomata, the openings that sponsor upward water flow by controlling transpiration. But during the winter months when water is frozen and unavailable and cold temperatures inhibit growth, the leaves are no longer useful. In fact, they become a liability, because they permit loss of precious water reserves through transpiration. Thus it is beneficial to the plant as a whole to sacrifice its leaves during periods of cold.

The primary stimulus for abscission is shorter days. Deciduous trees are sensitive to the amount of daily sunlight they receive. As the length of the day gradually decreases in the autumn months, chemical changes are triggered within the tree. Growth-promoting hormones such as *auxin* are reduced, while *ethylene*, a gas that rapidly ages plant tissues, increases.

One site of ethylene-induced aging is at the base of the stalk where the leaf connects to the stem (Figure 49). Some cells in this region weaken and separate, forming a gap that gradually separates the leaf from the stem. This process is amplified by adjacent cells that swell with water under the influence of ethylene. These swollen cells increase the pressure on the separating zone, causing more rapid deterioration and subsequent detachment of the leaf.

Ethylene also affects cells within the leaf. As photosynthetic cells begin to die, chlorophyll molecules break down rapidly, draining the leaves of their green color. When this occurs, other compounds that are normally invisible under the dominating green chlorophyll are exposed. These pigments, such as xanthophyll, carotene, and anthocyanin reflect various mixtures of yellow, orange, and red light, giving the expiring leaves their brilliant colors.

Finally the abscission zone separates completely, sending the brilliant leaves cascading to the ground. The plant is now dormant and remains inactive until the spring when hormones trigger the growth of new leaves and another cycle of growth resumes. This system of annual leaf replacement allows deciduous trees to flourish in climates of seasonal change, taking advantage of warm spring and summer months to grow and reproduce, then shutting down through the bitter cold of winter.

Figure 49
ABSCISSION:
Specialized cells (see inset) within the leaf stem separate, causing the leaf to die and change color.

© Christopher C. Bain

FOREST FIRES USEFUL?

WE DO NOT USUALLY THINK of forest fires as natural phenomena. But the fact is that fires have swept through wooded regions on a fairly regular basis, probably since the first forests arose many thousands of years ago. In fact, the ecology of forest regions is closely tied to the occasional burning of some areas. Let's examine the effect of fire on the many types of plant life that inhabit wooded areas. Then we will consider how our management of forest environments has altered the nature and impact of forest fires.

By examining the scars left on the inner rings of very old trees, scientists can determine the frequency and severity of fires in the past. This record shows that mild fires confined to burning along the ground were a regular occurrence in North American forests at least since the late 1600s—as far back as can be studied. This pattern was interrupted in the early 1900s, when wide-scale intervention of wild fires began.

Because fire is a regular part of forest communities, many of the plants have adapted to its presence. The dominant trees such as various species of pine and fir are covered with very thick bark on their trunks, which protects the inner tissues from damage. These trees also survive ground fires because of their height. The more susceptible branches and needles are high enough to escape the ravaging flames below.

Some shrubs, grasses, and small trees that are not tall enough to fully escape burning demonstrate another type of adaptation. When damaged by fire, these plants respond by sending out a torrent of new sprouts. Thus fire actually stimulates the proliferation of these species.

Another effect of fire has consequences for the forest community as a whole. In an area that has not experienced fire for many years, the lower branches of trees form a blanket over the forest floor, blocking sunlight and preventing growth of new trees (Figure 50). Ground fires effectively clear away these lower branches and open up the area for new growth. Even in regions where the lower branches of large trees have been previously cleared, many years without fire results in overcrowding of smaller shrubs and bushes. Eventually a few species dominate so that the variety of life forms is reduced. After a fire, the open, burned region is available for habitation by many new species. Thus, the diversity of plant life is usually greater in a particular area a few years after a fire than before.

Some plants have evolved to the point that their reproductive cycle is dependent on fire. Several members of the group *Ceanothus,* a group of western shrubs, produce seeds that are encased in an extremely hard outer coat. In this condition, the seeds are incapable of sprouting. The heat of a

The destruction caused by a bushfire such as this in South Africa's Hluhuwe Game Preserve can also have beneficial effects.

fire, however, causes the hard coat to open, after which the seed can germinate and grow, provided water is available.

Another example of this dependency of plants on fire is displayed by some types of evergreens. The cones of these species are sealed shut by a hard resin, preventing the seeds inside from escaping into the ground. This resin can only be melted by the high temperature of a fire, which opens the cones and releases the seeds. The cones can remain sealed for many years until a fire initiates the reproductive process.

In these instances, activation of the seeds of "fire species" is coordinated with the time when the ground is most likely to be open for seedlings to survive. In addition, the burnt remains of plants from a fire make a nutrient-rich base to sustain new plants. Thus, fire often promotes the renewal of forest regions, clearing away old plant life and preparing the terrain for new growth.

In the early 1900s when people began large-scale regulation of wilderness areas in the United States, forest fires became a national enemy. The prevailing attitude was to prevent and extinguish all forest fires, not realizing their possible benefits. This led to the buildup of fire-fighting programs, which cost more than $300 million every year. As a result of this effort, the regular cycle of clearing by natural ground fires was largely halted.

In unregulated regions, occasional wildfires consume the dead leaves and pine needles before they build up extensively.

Figure 50
GROUND CLEARING
BY FOREST FIRES:
Long periods without
fire lead to overcrowd-
ing and prevent new
growth. A ground fire
clears out brush and the
lower branches of trees,
providing space for new
and varied species
to grow.

For the most part, the limited fuel sponsors small ground fires, which clear brush, leave tall trees standing, and usually burn themselves out after covering a small area. But when massive forest areas are not visited by fire for many years, the debris piles up and dries out to form a thick layer of combustible material. At this stage, only one kind of fire is possible: a super hot "cone fire," which incinerates everything over thousands of acres (or hectares), including the tall trees. Wilderness areas stripped by such cone fires do not recover quickly: Even the hard seeds of fire species are destroyed by the extreme heat.

In recent years, more ecological-minded attitudes are beginning to prevail. Decision makers are accepting the fact that preventing all wildfires is ultimately detrimental to the environment. Some forest services now allow fires in certain locations to burn without intervening and have even instituted programs of controlled burns to prevent buildup of debris in dense areas. Fire-fighting services will always be important to prevent spread of large fires into valuable timber lands and to protect wooded areas that contain homes and other buildings, but a comprehensive strategy that takes into account the natural role of forest fires is now the accepted policy.

By observing and studying the natural phenomena around us, we begin to know planet earth and how it operates. And when we understand our world, we gain insight into how we should use and enjoy our natural resources without permanently damaging our fragile environment.

For Additional Reading

Editorial Staff of Time-Life Books. *Voyage Through the Universe.* Alexandria, Virginia: Time-Life Books, 1988.

Harris, Norman (editor). *New Larousse Encyclopedia of Earth.* Feltham, Middlesex, England: Hamlin House, 1972.

Hurlbut, Cornelius S., Jr. (editor). *The Planet We Live On.* New York: Harry N. Abram, Inc., 1976.

Kondo, Herbert (editor). *The New Book of Popular Science.* USA: Grolier Inc., 1982.

Pringle, Laurence. *Being a Plant.* New York: Thomas Y. Crowell, 1983.

Ramsey, William L., et. al. *Modern Earth Science.* New York: Holt, Rinehart and Winston, Inc., 1969.

Whipple, Fred L. *Orbiting the Sun.* Cambridge, Massachusetts: Harvard University Press, 1981.

© Rod Planck/Dembinsky Photo Association